@urFRENZ

@urFRENZ

Jeff Phillips

TINSEL ROAD BOOKS
Santa Monica, California

This book is a work of fiction. Any references to historical events, real people, or real locales are used fictitiously. Other names, characters, places, and incidents are the product of the author's imagination, and any resemblance to actual events or locales or persons, living or dead, is entirely coincidental.

Books may be purchased for educational, business or sales promotional use. For information, please write: Special Markets Department, Tinsel Road Books, a division of Quattro Media, 171 Pier Avenue, Ste 328, Santa Monica, CA 90405 USA.

FIRST EDITION

Library of Congress Cataloging-in-Publication-Data is available on file.

ISBN: 978-1-936573-04-2

americanforests.org

GL🌐BAL
RE🍃LEAF

Tinsel Road Books, in association with Global ReLeaf, will plant two trees for each tree used in the manufacturing of this book. Global ReLeaf is an international campaign by American Forests, the nation's oldest nonprofit conservation organization and a world leader in planting trees for environmental restoration.

10 9 8 7 6 5 4 3 2 1

DEDICATION

To my wife, Annette, for never doubting me, always supporting me. You are my best friend, and my great love. Thank you for showing me that being a husband and father are the most important things in life.

To Sean McNamara and David Brookwell who were there in the beginning. When we were wide-eyed production assistants lying about our mileage in order to make rent.

To Charles Segars for continually helping me to live the dream. And carrying me along the way.

To Christina Welsh for being a great writer, an even better friend.

To Max Enscoe for making me a better writer. And teaching me the meaning of the word mensch.

And to my manager, Jim Strader, for suffering my quirks and anxieties. And never giving me dumb notes on my scripts. If every writer-director's reps were like you and trusted their talent, the industry would be a better, more creative place.

TABLE OF CONTENTS

FOREWORD

Jeff Phillips is a master. He writes. He directs. He produces. And, the greatest gift of all, he teaches. He gives back to University Students what he has learned, created and more. The definition of a master is somebody who is highly skilled in a craft and is qualified to teach. That is Jeff. A master filmmaker. I'm also blessed to call him my friend.

I've known Jeff since college and he always makes me laugh. With his wit and comic timing, he could be a stand-up comedian. He can keep a group of people entertained for hours. When I'm having a bad day, he knows just how to cheer me up. He always asks about my family. He listens. He advises. Always saying the most inappropriate thing at the right time that is always appropriate to put a smile on my face.

Jeff is the most passionate person I know when it comes to writing. He knew he wanted to be a writer ever since we met back in undergrad. And he wrote and wrote. And he would re-write and re-write. Every few months he had a new script to show me. A Fort Knox Heist script. An Armageddon script. A balls out comedy. A horror film. I truly think he is the most prolific writer I know. He loves writing with his whole being.

We have worked together a great deal. He has written some of the best family movies, and I got the chance to direct some of them. He's a walking encyclopedia of any film, ever made. He researches more than anyone I know which gives his films an authenticity that few have. Jeff can write fast. "Hey Jeff, we need 44 episodes of a new show written in a month." Jeff responds, "No problem." "Jeff, the good news is I got this great movie about a Grizzly Bear. The bad news is we got 3 days to re-write it. Jeff's response – "No problem." Then he delivers the goods. And they're damn good.

When I saw the directors cut of "@urFrenz," I was literally blown away. Jeff has made the jump from writer, to Writer/Director. I was put under his spell for a couple of hours. When I was done watching it, and after a few moments of being incredibly jealous, I realized what an artist Jeff has become. He could show his vision of a deeply personal story and pack a potent punch of emotion and stylized storytelling. His direction of actors, his camera movement and editing reminds me of the great European Auteur. His shading of his complex characters mirror real life experiences. The tragedy is realistic and shocking and makes you ponder where our society is going. Yet at the end, there is hope. I just Love "@urFrenz" and am so proud to have a small part in it.

Jeff Phillips is a master filmmaker. He writes. He directs. He produces. I'm blessed to call him my friend.

- Sean MacNamara, 2011

INTRODUCTION

The following is a record of what it took to get the first film I have written, produced and directed onto the screen. Read it and you will learn...

1) What it takes to guide a story from the idea to the page to full script

2) What are the pros and cons of self-financing your film

3) How to produce an independent narrative feature film from pre-production through distribution

Filmmaking is not brain surgery, but to do it well you need to respect and master the craft. It also helps to have a little talent, luck and timing on your side. For me, "@urFRENZ" is the perfect marriage of all three. It's also a reminder that the best stories are your own.

@urFRENZ

THE JOURNAL

The idea for an original screenplay takes time to gestate. "@urFRENZ" is no exception. When I get an idea for a story, I create a folder on my Mac and keep adding to it. I literally have thousands of these folders. Some containing half beat out ideas, others that are completely fleshed out and just waiting to be written. This was a story that evolved over the course of the last decade. It began back in 2000, during the run up to the Presidential election.

*The below are compiled from my original notes. I've updated the text where appropriate, but otherwise the notes remain unedited. My apologies for the shifts in tense and additional butchering of the English language.

Warning: Spoilers ahead!

April 2000

I dropped in on political chat rooms on AOL. My hope was to engage in a meaningful political dialogue. Instead, what I discovered was a cesspool of anger and hate. People responding with profanity-laced tirades born of ideology, partisanship and ignorance. Saying things they'd never have the courage to say in public without the aid of alcohol.

I make a mental note that the internet, while having the ability to bring out the best in people could also bring out the worst. I start thinking about a scenario where a story plays out in a chat room arena. Maybe a stage play where two people on computers are separated by a single wall. They voice their chat room comments as they type. What if the set was an office floor comprised of cubicles? Several people interacting pleasantly enough during the course of their workday, but at night unknowingly chatting with each other and revealing their dark sides.

November 2003

I watch Gus Van Sant's film "Elephant," which won the Palme d'Or at the Cannes Film Festival. I'm blown away by this powerful film. The film details the events surrounding a school shooting much like Columbine. Several aspects of the film stand out for me including:

-Low budget, no name stars. Without a name, the audience has no idea who lives or dies. Makes them more engaged in the story.

-The dialogue feels more improvised than scripted, adding to the authenticity of the film.

-Harris Savides' brilliant cinematography

-The use of long tracking shots. Removes the necessity for cutting between medium and close shots, which would lend an artificial quality to such realistic subject matter.

-The setting is a character. The use of the lengthy tracking shots across the huge campus dwarfs the students making them feel more like prisoners at times than students. I had a moment while watching the film where I remembered reading about Columbine and wondering why the students had a hard time getting away from the shooters. By using the tracking shots, Van Sant weaves you in and out of the school, its many hallways and floors, like you're caught in a maze built by Daedalus. When the shooting starts later in the film, you understand why the kids could get trapped. The acoustics of the building also make it hard to discern where the gunshots are coming from.

-The long tracking shots make the fictional school setting feel like a haunted house. They remind me of the Overlook Hotel in Kubrick's "The Shining."

-Start thinking about a dramatic piece centering on this age group, the angst and rage they experience.

December 2003

Paris Hilton's sex tape is released right before the premiere of her reality show "The Simple Life." Hard to tell if she's legitimately embarrassed or capitalizing on the latest way to self-promote. Gives rise to the old show biz adage, "there's no such thing as bad publicity."

Consider the issue of privacy in the internet age. Could you blackmail a former lover with an embarrassing video? And given the speed and access to untold millions worldwide, would you ever be able to live down such an episode? What's the legality of publicly exposing something clearly meant to be private?

January 2005

I've spent a decade being hired to write genre material for the major studios and various production companies. Initially, I landed an agent by writing a personal drama about race relations and gentrification during the mid 1970's era of white-flight in Southern California. Ever since, I'd written nothing but genre: from big budget actioners and science fiction to horror, suspense thrillers and family comedies. I need to write something that matters.

I apply to grad school at Chapman University in Orange, CA, to study Creative Writing in the hopes of rediscovering the types of stories that got me interested in writing as a child. The campus is ideal due to its proximity to my home in the OC. (I will study under Jim Blaylock and Tim Powers, two brilliant writers who were mentored by Philip K. Dick, of whose work I'm a huge fan.)

After the success of the Disney film of Meg Cabot's epistolary novel, "The Princess Diaries," I want to consider a novel, possibly a screenplay, based around emails and texts. …the short message prose format is a natural for screenwriters. I start thinking about a film based entirely around e-communication. A fast paced narrative to match society's hyperspeed attention span. Maybe an impressionistic film that moves from user to user, one device to the next. It could take place in a single day like Richard Linklater's "Slacker."

But is it visual enough? Who wants to watch a movie comprised of people sitting behind computer screens or staring into their phones?

June 2005

I commit to a dual degree program—the MFA plus an MA in English. It's a three-year program. My undergraduate degree was a dual emphasis in Screenwriting and Film Production. As a writer, I've always felt lacking for an English degree. Like I missed out on a critical rite of passage.

I talk to Joe Slowensky, the Screenwriting Chair at Dodge College, Chapman's film school, about teaching an occasional class in screenwriting. He's a great guy, a former writer and network exec, and tells me he'll consider me for a class in '06. The relationships I make here will be integral to the making of "@urFRENZ."

July 2005

A woman in South Korea rides a subway with her dog. After the pooch does his business on the train, she makes no attempt to clean it up. A rider on the same train takes of picture of the incident with his camera phone and posts it online. She is labeled Dog Poop Girl, and within days her identity is revealed. She is unable to live down the public humiliation that follows and reportedly has to relocate.

The speed with which she is outed is astonishing. It's an example of internet vigilantism. Coordinated attacks to bring someone to justice in the public eye for a perceived act. But does the punishment fit the crime?

August 2005

My first Grad school class is a Seminar in Literary Analysis: Private Writing and Public Reading. The main focus is on epistolary fiction, writing that positions the reader as a voyeur, someone transgressing the writer's private life. The course also features "blackmail" fiction, which is concerned with the right and wrong of publicizing the truth about someone. The professor is Dr. Logan Esdale, a Dickinson scholar and one of the brightest people I've ever met. The lectures on Bram Stoker's epistolary novel *Dracula*, and rights to privacy issues in other texts will go a long way towards developing the themes for the script for "@urFRENZ."

August 2006

I begin teaching a course in screenwriting at Chapman University at their impressive state-of-the-art production facility on the Dodge Campus. They have a great staff and everything needed to make professional quality films.

September 2006

The LA Times runs an article on Lonelygirl15, a hit web based series. The show features a video-blog format with a teen girl talking into the camera about various aspects of her life. Posted on youtube, the show became an internet sensation, partly due to the mystery of whether her revelations are real or not. Turns out, the show is a hoax, the fictional brainchild of a filmmaker from Marin County, CA. The fifteen year old is actually a nineteen-year-old actress from New Zealand.

November 2006-April 2008

My daughter, Aida, enters junior high. She's a relatively normal teenage girl whose interests include soccer and Hilary Duff's music. But a couple months into the seventh grade she grows quieter, and angrier. Soon, she's listening to darker, emo-music and dressing in black. We come to find out through her peers and other parents that she is the victim of bullying.

Aida asks for a MySpace account, my wife and I discuss the pros and cons of it. Eventually, we acquiesce but only after letting her know that we will monitor her site from time to time. She agrees. We routinely check her pages and, other than her music interests, we find nothing exceptional.

Months later, her moods have gotten darker, she is less communicative. We take her to see a psychologist. The initial diagnosis is mild Asberger's – her inability to read social cues is noted.

On April 19th, 2007, I got a phone call through my wife. Aida is in the hospital. I drive to the UCI Pediatric Psychiatric department in Orange. Her junior high school called earlier because of a note she had written. The note had blood on it and described how she had been cutting herself. The friend at school that received the note had the good sense to hand it over to the school staff.

I arrive to find Aida medicated and wearing a hospital gown and under medication. I'm stunned by what I see: she has lengthy cuts up and down her legs. She looks like she ran through a field of barbed wire. She also has several cuts on her wrists, her arm and her chest. I don't even know how to react to this. I'd heard of self-mutilation, what some refer to as "cutters," but have no practical connection to it. This is a sociological phenomenon that's been growing steadily among the populous for the past two decades. We learn that 80-90% of self-mutilators are adolescent teenage girls.

The doctors tell us she's stable for now. How could this happen right under our noses? My wife is a full time mother to our five children, and I write out of the home. We start doing the math. She hid the cuts on her left wrist by wearing an ever-accumulating number of bracelets on the one arm. She's never worn dresses, so the pants covered up the legs. She's here for the next 7-10 days, while we look into treatment options. One of which is a residential treatment facility in Utah, where the stay can last for several months to well over a year. (This is the answer to the line in the film where Catharine comments on Utah being worse than death. Most troubled teens know, it's the nation's capital for long-term care.)

During this period and up until press, cyberbullying and sexting stories become part of the language and a larger part of the zeitgeist. Ryan Halligan, Megan Meier, Emily Moore, Jesse Logan, Tyler Clementi to name a few. I know there's a story here. Somebody has to address this on a larger platform than daytime TV.

We start looking for clues to Aida's bullying. This leads to stricter monitoring of her social networking site. We discover she's opened another account where she communicates more closely with others. We find evidence of cyberbullying during these chats. We start paying attention to and researching like stories about cyberbullying and the related topic of sexting in the media. We learn the language of these sessions, how kids confess, conceal, gossip and outright lie about their peers. We uncover adults posing as "friends," some of who are undoubtedly parents, based on their clumsy attempts at chatting up others. While we are guilty of "spying" on our daughter, we do not enter into the conversation. (Though the writer in me starts imagining scenes where I do respond to the vitriol.) We discuss the issue at length with the various psychiatric professionals treating our daughter. They assure us that in extreme cases like this, we can't be watchful enough. We do let Aida know that we are carefully monitoring her account and draw up a written contract to better enforce the guidelines for her use of the sites.

November 2008

Abraham Biggs, a 19-year-old college student in Miami, commits suicide online in front of a live audience. Using a webcam, he linked to a bodybuilding site, Justin.tv, that served as the host site and allowed for users to post comments. The scene played out over several hours while some computer users spurred him on.

I start thinking about the feasibility of a film about this topic. About the distance between the web audience and someone attempting to kill themselves on line.

December 2008

I start beating out the idea for a fictional film about someone committing suicide before a live online audience. What I'm thinking:

-Who's my protagonist? Must be someone who tries to stop it, though maybe not initially. In "The River's Edge" Keanu Reeves plays a character who is at first apathetic about revealing the location of the dead female classmate, but wrestles with his conscious over the course of the film about the right thing to do.

-Need a group who eggs on the person to commit suicide. Much like the group that egged on the rapists in "The Accused."

-Because of the worldwide access to the site, I think it might be best to focus on one town. Maybe the victim's own community, people that know him or her.

January 2009

I realize the story I need to write deals with cyberbullying. I've spent the past 2 years living in the world of internet parenting. The subject matter has not been tackled on film. I want this to be the first. I need to address this subject matter in a way that will call attention to it, but without being preachy.

My daughter has stopped cutting. I talk to her and my wife about the story I'm thinking of writing. It will be fictional, but I want their blessing. Both feel a story about the subject matter might help prevent cyberbullying and the related emotions that lead to self-harm or suicide.

I start compiling notes on character and beating out an outline borne of their actions. I decide I want the focus to be on two teenage girls and their families.

February 2009

I'm thinking about going beyond the script stage and making the movie myself. Writing, directing and producing. It's the only way to guarantee the film will ever get made. The story is too personal to me and I do not want to subject it to the development process around town. For starters, the major studios are averse to original dramas as if they were the Avian Flu. They don't understand how to market them, meaning they can't guarantee a profit that will "move the needle." Friends have been on me to direct for years, maybe now is the time.

Unfortunately, this also means I'll have to finance the picture on my own. Only way to guarantee control over the script and the look of the picture. I wonder how my wife feels about taking equity out of our home.

March 2009

I'm going to make the picture with new or young filmmakers. During the screenwriting and production classes I've taught at Chapman and Loyola Marymount, I'm constantly amazed at how much incoming students already know about film. Film schools exploded in the 1990's. Thanks to the internet, DIY filmmaking information is easily accessible. And channels like youtube, allow for anyone to post their own homemade shorts. Simply put, today's film students walk in the door knowing more about filmmaking than my generation did upon graduating from college.

A benefit of working with new filmmakers, recent grads is in part what they don't know: the business aspect of Hollywood. They haven't been beaten down by development execs or production types constantly telling them "no." Everything with them is a "why not" and a possibility. They are also more up-to-date in technology upgrades in film and digital media.

Cost is also a factor. I cannot afford to shoot my movie with union crews, not when I'm funding out of pocket. New filmmakers rates are generally cheaper, though sites like craigslist are full of talented experienced people willing to work for little to no pay. I decide I want to reach out to several top former students to work on my film. The opportunity to crew a feature a couple years out of film school can be a significant leg up in your career, one where opportunity and experience are a never ending catch-22. I've worked most of the positions on set during my own career in production and feel comfortable enough to handle any concerns that may arise.

I start to make contact with former students, letting them know I may be shooting a picture over the summer. First I need to get off my ass and write the script.

April 2009

The outline is complete. I spend the month concentrating on issues related to theme. This story is about something and I want it to work on several levels. Of paramount importance to me, is to tell the tale with as little exposition as possible. Making expositional dialogue sound like actual dialogue always feels like half the battle of rewriting. In television, you're not constantly having to introduce people. But in film, you've got roughly 2 hours to introduce the world in your story and everyone in it. I read somewhere that Humphrey Bogart once said that whenever he has to deliver exposition he hopes there are camels fucking in the background so the audience doesn't fall asleep. I don't have the budget for camels, so I better write lean.

May 1-15, 2009

I start writing the script. My usual process involves locking myself in my office and writing as quickly as possible to get a draft done. This is often referred to in the industry as the "puke draft." Meaning you puke it up quickly to get it onto the page. Once you've finished the first draft, the real writing can begin: the rewrite process. I liken first drafts to a sculptor's lump of clay. You know you're creating something, but not entirely certain what it will look like; it's a process of shaping and reshaping the material until it reveals itself in full.

I bang out the script in fifteen days. This a week sooner than I usually finish a first draft. I'll continue to tinker with the script up to and through production. This time, however, I know that 95% of what I have will remain. Maybe because I'd lived with the story so long, I feel like the script wrote itself. Sometimes it just comes.

The working title is "Mean."

PRODUCTION NOTES

PREP:

May 28, 2009

Meeting with Kelley Logan, her sister Jamie Ford and thirteen year old niece Shaena Brun. Kelley is an exceptional former student and an all around great human being. I had mentioned the film to her and my desire to talk with as many teens on the film's subject matter before shooting. She arranged for me to come to their place and talk to her niece about teenagers and social networking.

Shaena has already prepared a lengthy glossary of popular internet terms she uses to communicate online. She logs on to her account and lets me be a fly on the wall. Feel like a trespassing voyeur, but the observation is invaluable. I will apply the knowledge gained to my script while rewriting.

June 1, 2009

I hire a Producer, Jana Winternitz. She's a former student, bright, engaging with a good knowledge of independent film, and an intuitive sense of story. She's also hungry to prove herself, both as a producer and an actor. Back in April, she heard I was looking to shoot a film over the summer and wanted to be involved in a producing capacity. We met mid-May and she really impressed.

I tell her I want a minimum of producers on this flick. She's welcome to hire an assistant, even bring on a co-producer, but that's it. I don't like the idea of handing over a producer credit to anyone and everyone. It has the effect of watering down the position and reducing the credibility of the job.

We'll be shooting on a low budget, which can be a blessing. While you're limited on size and scope, the dollar limit forces you to strip the story down and focus on what is essential to telling the tale. If the tech credits are good, the audience won't care whether you shoot for 1 million or 10 million. Provided, of course, the story and performances ring true.

First date of shooting is set for July 20th. Plan is to shoot for three 5-day weeks in town.

June 2, 2009

Jana asks about the possibility for shooting on the RED ONE camera, the best digital camera on the market. It's the closest thing to shooting on film. I've heard all the arguments for shooting on film, but it's a dying art form. Shooting on digital is more cost effective and will allow us to move faster. I tell her to look into it. I'd planned to shoot with Billy Peake, a talented young filmmaker, on his Sony PMW EX3 Camera. He's also got a steadicam rig for it, which I could put to good use during lengthy tracking shots I have planned. If we go with the RED, I'll have to use a DP who has worked with that camera.

June 5, 2009

Jana scouts her former school, Torrey Pines High, emails me shots of the campus. It's beautiful, spacious with some interesting architecture. They seem keen on letting us film there. Only drawback is the location: San Diego county. This puts us outside the 30-mile studio zone, meaning distant location. We'll have to pay more for things like travel, mileage, etc.. Still, this is our chief location.

June 8, 2009

Virtually Exposed Productions, LLC is established as the official production company for the picture.

We start calling other high schools around Southern California to obtain permission to shoot. Thanks to state budget cuts and other funding shortages, scores of public schools are having to eliminate summer school courses. Meaning little to no staff will be around between mid-June through August. Getting hold of the people in charge proves difficult. Messages are left and when calls are returned the news is not good for the reasons previously mentioned. Of all the years to film something in a high school, this is the worst.

I tell Jana to chase Melissa Leo for the role of Debbie. I'm a big fan of her performance in Frozen River. Working with a name means more money, and working around their schedule. If she says yes, I'll find the money. But working with unknowns has its advantages. The audience won't be taken out of the story as recognition of known talent often does. Regardless, I'm shooting this movie now. On my time and schedule.

June 11, 2009

Jana meets with the Screen Actor's Guild to begin paperwork for our film. It's a no-brainer. Talent is everything. Don't overlook talented SAG-eligible actors, but if you can afford, go SAG.

June 12, 2009

We begin casting up in Hollywood. The place is the Space Station at 1258 Highland.

Jana has handled the difficult process of weeding through headshots and resumes. She's forwarded the best candidates to me for approval. During sessions, she reads along with many of the talent. Her line delivery is excellent and a huge help during read-throughs.

Notes from Casting session 1: Najarra Townsend, a slender, attractive brunette nails her first read for the part of Madison. She has serious acting chops having acted in Miranda July's Cannes Film Festival Winner, "Me and You and Everyone We Know."

Aaron Fenton is a strong possibility for Catharine. I saw her in a short and was impressed with her ability.

Bree Essrig reads for the part of Catharine, but I'm now thinking of her as a possible Hannah, Catharine's best friend.

CaroleAnne Johnson nailed the part of Beth. She brought her instincts as a mom to the part and gave a fantastic audition. I have no doubts she can play the role.

We see candidates for Debbie, arguably the most important role alongside Catharine's. She's the primary antagonist. While the film is a serious indie-drama, the plot also functions a thriller. And good thrillers live and die with the antagonist.

June 13, 2009

I speak with a good friend from undergrad days, Anthony Cistaro. He's a fantastic actor, most known for his recurring role of Henri on "Cheers," and for playing Kenneth Irons on the short lived series, "WitchBlade." He gives me a tip on someone who'd be great for the part of Debbie. Her name is Gayla Goehl, an actor from NY who now works and teaches her craft in Los Angeles. I love the thought of casting Anthony to play the part of her husband in the film, but he's recently moved his family up to San Francisco and is unavailable.

I hire Zach Anderson as my editor. He comes highly recommended from Harry Cheney and Paul Seydor, both industry vets and professors at Chapman. I knew him as a former student who took screenwriting classes from me to better understand the nature of his own craft of editing. I'd seen some of his work and was very impressed with his style of cutting.

I review the script with a friend of mine, Teri Hillis, a highly respected script clearance professional. We discuss potential legal issues regarding my script regarding everything from a title search to brand placement. This is a must for every filmmaker before production and you'll need it to secure Errors & Omission Insurance.

June 19, 2009

More casting. Jessica Lee Rose gives a great reading for Catharine. Irony of ironies: she's LonelyGirl15, the former internet sensation. If we cast her, that alone will make for a good story. File it under kismet.

Gayla Goehl auditions. She's fantastic. If we don't go with name talent, she's the front-runner for the part.

June 23, 2009

Torrey Pines scout. The campus is really impressive in person. Has a great look to it, one that I can capitalize on visually.

June 30, 2009

More casting. So far, I like the following:

Gayla Goehl for Debbie. Jessica Lee Rose for Catharine. Najarra Townsend for Madison. CaroleAnne Howard for Beth.

July 1, 2009

Bad news: we will not be allowed to film at Torrey Pines High School. The Los Angeles Unified School District was upset about a June GQ article where Sacha Baron Cohen appeared in some questionable photos with members of the football team from a Van Nuys High School. The stunt was for "Bruno," starring Cohen as the titular character. The result had a trickle down effect on other southern California area high schools. Apparently, we are a casualty.

Three weeks out and we lose our principal location. As Bill Murray's characters said in "Stripes": *and then depression set it.*

July 2, 2009

Storyboards completed. Billy and I have been shooting photo-boards with a still camera. I like them better than drawings because of the depth and realism. Amanda Young, a writer and former student, is a big help in volunteering to double for Catharine in the shots.

July 3, 2009

Budget completed with help from Rachel Skidmore, a talented young producer. We had talked previously about working together to develop original material. She has some good suggestions for cost-cutting in the OC. I push production back a week. We'll now begin shooting Monday, July 27.

July 4, 2009

Still not seeing what I need to see for the parts of Jacob and Brandon.

We offer the role of Beth to CaroleAnne. She accepts.

July 5, 2009

Billy is able to get in contact with nearby Orange High School and they seem amenable to working with us. We schedule a meeting and scout for later.

Get word that Melissa Leo respectively passes.

July 6, 2009

Matthew Sullivan is brought on as Associate Producer. He'll function as the UPM. He's also done location work in the OC, and he and Billy will work to nail down our locations.

July 8, 2009

We offer the role of Madison to Najarra. She accepts.

We offer the role of Catharine to Jessica Lee Rose. She is excited about the role.

We offer the role of Debbie to Gayla. She accepts.

Orange High is a go for us to shoot at. I decide we'll shoot the entire film in the OC, with as many locations in or near Orange/Santa Ana as possible.

July 10, 2009

I see a cellphone ad in Entertainment Weekly. Motorola encourages its users to "Out-Thumb Your Friends." The ad features 4 teen-types discussing how they text: "I text about rumored hookups...alleged flare-ups...speculated breakups...all my texts are made up." The cavalier approach to spreading potentially harmful gossip tells me I'm on the right track.

July 14, 2009

We launch our Kickstarter account on line to raise additional funds for shooting on The RED camera. The fundraising site is recommended by Michael Gallagher, who is close to Jana. He's a director-writer-producer, who runs a popular sketch comedy website, TotallySketch.com. He proves himself invaluable in casting suggestions and ends up donating the money to put us over the top to meet our Kickstarter goal. He will also contribute several creative suggestions that will be incorporated into the film, from prep through postproduction.

He will come on as Co-Producer before shooting begins.

July 15, 2009

We continue negotiations between Jessica Lee Rose and her agency. We don't have a deal yet.

July 16, 2009

Billy finds World Star Realty in Orange. Looks great for Debbie's office. We're still on course to shoot on 7/27.

I meet with J. Soren Viuf, a Chapman alum. I've met with several DP candidates up to this point. I like his reel, and he's also worked with other members of the crew. Something clicks with him and he's hired on. He's a real thinking man's cinematographer. Over the course of the next week I'll discuss the look of the picture with him:

-I want to establish a neo-realist feel. Fluid camera movement.

-Long tracking shots in some sequences to put the audience in the shoes of the actors.

-Catharine's movement into online fantasy should feel almost dream like.

-Shoot handheld (but not shaky cam) to emphasize realism. Camera wandering at times to give a pseudo documentary feeling.

-Though the script calls for scores of SCREENSHOTS featuring text on computers, cells, blackberry's, we will not be looking at boring blank screens. The content of the screens will feature visual and interactive content, which will also be used as portals in and out of shots. They will be part of the overall visual strategy.

-I want to treat the social networking site as a character. Maybe shoot it dirty with Catharine in the shot. She is connecting more with the computer and its avatars than with real people.

-We could have blue light from the screen on her face and use the screen itself as an eyelight. As the film goes on the blue light continues to look more and more sickly, and the screen eyelight becomes even more prominent, as if it's starting to devour her soul. Have the light play off her face slightly. Probably no more than that in this first scene.

-We could make outside appear very claustrophobic, not open, by shooting scenes like this with a really long lens to collapse the space, or a really wide lens to make it look odd and uncomfortable. In addition, we could use a shallow depth of field to add to this effect. Though…

-We could open up the outside world a little to give the audience a breather. While Madison is playing soccer, for example, we could keep the framing wide and loose, and keep the depth of field deeper than it has been.

-Other notes on character… keeping Catharine in a clean single but have the Mom's shots dirty could go to the theme of isolation. This goes to a visual motif we could use throughout the film. In some ways, the teens in this world are very isolated from interpersonal relationships in the real world, as they live so much on the internet. We could think about, especially in Catharine and Madison's case, isolating them in clean singles on their close-ups. Whereas on the adults' close-ups, the children are dirty in the frames, because they are trying to and unable to connect.

-Shoot through windows/glass to play off the walls that separate kids and parents in the film.

When we're done discussing the look of the picture, I tell him my chief concern will be on the talent. I have no desire to spend the film in video village looking at performances through another screen.

I provide my keys with a notebook of photoboards for most of the script. Each scene will contain my notes on how I want to convey the scene visually in connection with character, story and theme. Each shot will contain my notes on camera movement , lenses, lighting.

Films we screen as inspirations for the look of the film: Elephant, Bully, Thirteen, Half Nelson and United 93.

July 17, 2009

Bad news part II: The Orange County School District tells us we cannot use any of the students from summer school. There is no debate on the issue. There go my extras, something I need badly to sell the authenticity of the school. This also means shuffling our shooting schedule, which was based around shooting while school was in session.

I speak with SK Johnson, Orange High's principal. He'll allow us to snap a few crowd shots when summer school is letting out, but that's all he can do.

We also get a list from Jessica Lee Rose's agency about scheduling conflicts in July and August. Her preference is to shoot primarily on the weekends. This will require considerable rescheduling on our part to make this work.

Michael Gallagher hooks us up with a contact for internet design. Her name is Jessica Lares and she lives in Texas. I send her the script with a laundry list of everything we need the site to do. I want a working site for the shoot that will work in real time. When completed, I will have the cast members create their own webpages for their characters to be used in the film. Jessica couldn't be nicer. Gives us a huge break on cost for the design.

July 20, 2009

We live in SoCal and the nights don't start until after 8. I reslugged some scenes to minimize shooting at night. I'll discuss day for night options with Soren in the next couple of days.

Profanity, sex and violence affect both MPAA ratings as well as those in TV. My film has some profanity and I'll cover the lines both onscreen and wild. The difference between PG-13 and R affects your audience and needs to be addressed before shooting.

Rehearsals begin tonight and through the rest of the week at Space Station.

July 22, 2009

Bad news part III: We get an email from Jessica Lee Rose at 3A. She's ankling the project for personal reasons. File this under *things I wish I knew yesterday.*

We're five days out from the start of principal photography without a lead actor. I bemoan the fates for about 15 minutes, then move on. Forward movement is paramount.

July 23, 2009

Script timing. We come in at around 98 minutes. Perfect.

I lock our shooting dates in with the insurance company. Sans stunts, guns, car chases and explosives, the cost for us runs only a few thousand.

I consider the runners up I'd previously met with for the role of Catharine, but I'm not completely sold.

July 24, 2009

Jana gets a lead on a potential Catharine from Michael Gallagher via a connection of his, Patrick O'Sullivan. She's going to meet with her tomorrow.

I tell Shannon Welch, the first AD, to shuffle the shooting schedule so we don't shoot Catharine's scenes the first couple of days. Shannon is from Chicago and has a steady but firm hand with the crew.

Good news. Jessica Lares delivers a fantastic working social networking site. Seeing it for the first time makes me realize I've got the wrong title. I talk about this with the key crew. It's official:

The new title is urFRENZ. (Note: later we will tweak the name to correspond to the Twitter account and retitle the picture "@urFRENZ.")

July 25, 2009

We have our production meeting with all the keys. Soren, Shannon, Matt Sullivan, Zach, Billy, Jana, Michael and our PD, Kristy McCaw.

I reiterate with the group what I'd already told them individually after first hiring them. Some of them I knew and worked with personally, others I'd seen examples of their talent. I talk to them about how I like to work. I don't want to be an autocrat on the set. One of my favorite quotes is from the former titan of advertising, David Ogilvy. "If each of us hires people who are smaller than we are, we shall become a company of dwarfs. But if each of us hires people who are bigger than we are, we shall become a company of giants." I feel the same way about my crew. I've hired them not to serve but to contribute. If my key creatives have thoughts about the story that will make a better picture, I want to hear about it. I remind them two things can kill a film. One is money, the other ego. Everything has to be in service to the film.

Jana tells me she really likes the actor she met with. Her name is Lily Holleman. I look at her headshot. It's a glamour shot, she looks too pretty for the part. While she has a strong dramatic background, what really stands out is her comedy work. She's worked with Tracey Ullman, one of the truly gifted comedic performers of all time. I'm just not seeing her for the role, but I trust Jana's instincts. I agree to meet Lily up in Hollywood the next day, the day before shooting. I tell Jana to let Lily know to dress down for our meeting. If she's too pretty, it will be harder for an audience to buy her as a social outcast.

Jana gives me a link to a role Lily played on the series "Southland." She's a junkie trying to gain custody of her child. I'm impressed.

July 26, 2009

I meet with Lily at the Coffee Bean & Tea Leaf in Hollywood on Sunset. She's pretty, but has dressed to downplay her attractive features. She's also slender and tiny, lending the appearance of someone who can disappear inside herself, a key component to the role. Her eyes are expressive, which will go a long way to establishing her vulnerability. She likes the script and feels a kinship to the character of Catharine.

We talk for a couple of hours, compare backgrounds. I tell her what I'm looking for from the part. We won't have time for any formal rehearsals beyond what time on the set allows. I tell her I feel good about her in the role. I call Jana and tell her to lock her down.

We now have a lead.

PRINCIPAL PHOTOGRAPHY July 27 - August 14

Before Production began, I told my four principal actresses that there were no "bitches" in the film. The driving force behind the plot involves rumors, gossip, and conversations in secret via social networking. Each of the women have defendable reasons for their actions:

-Catharine spreads the rumor about Madison because of a past slight. They used to be friends until Madison started to run with a popular crowd.

-Madison doesn't confront Catharine directly after the rumor, partly out of deep-rooted guilt for dumping her former friend. And like a large segment of her generation, the reliance on "faceless" communication via technology has hampered her ability to address her problems face to face. She responds with her own catty comments towards Catharine online. (Consider whether or not her boyfriend dumped her via a text message.)

-Debbie's interest in the online world begins with the best of intentions: she wants to protect her daughter. After learning that a schoolmate, and former friend, is spreading rumors about her, she becomes a grizzly mama. Her interest in Catharine, however, becomes an obsession, causing her to overlook her own daughter's depression.

-Beth walks the fine line between parenting her child's activities and invading her privacy. Her character is an amalgam of my wife and I during the two previous years we spent parenting our own daughter online. She wants to give Catharine her space, but is cognizant of the dangers lurking on the web. She's in a tough spot because her daughter has been diagnosed with a psychological disorder. This is never pinpointed in the film because diagnosing teens is incredibly complex. My own daughter's diagnosis ranged from depression to Asperger's syndrome to Bipolar disorder. Because Catharine is tight lipped and doesn't understand how to communicate what she's feeling with her, Beth is forced to snoop on her urFRENZ site to find out what's happening with her daughter.

With the exception of the grocery store scene, none of the characters from one family interact directly with the other in the script. I keep Gayla and Madison's rehearsals separate from those of Beth and Lily's characters to reflect their failure to confront their problems face to face. I want the grocery sequence between Gayla and Beth to feel like a traffic accident: a collision between two surprised parties.

When you're directing a film, it becomes all encompassing. It's 24/7 until you wrap. Sleep is an afterthought. The rapture could begin and still the only thing that matters is finishing the film. The director is accountable to everyone and the keys have your ear from the moment you wake. Because this was a low budget shoot and I'd be calling in a lot of favors, I kept to a five-day workweek and twelve-hour days. From previous experiences on set, I knew that having a full weekend to recharge would maximize crew productivity. And with the exception of one day when we went over schedule by fifteen minutes, we maintained an industry normal twelve-hour day the entire shoot.

At fifteen days, I knew we'd need to move quickly to get all of our planned setups. But I'd written the script to be production friendly and minimize locations. We had no stunts, no pyrotechnics, nothing that would be pulling serious time off the clock. Shooting everything in and around Orange County allowed us to keep company moves production friendly.

Day one: we're shooting the scenes in Debbie/Madison's house. First gaffe: Street sweeping day and someone neglected to do their job. We're forced to knock on neighbors' houses and beg to let us park in their driveways until sweeping is completed. If that's as bad as it gets, we're fine.

The first week of shooting goes great. It took a couple of days for the crew to get in sync, but after that things went smoothly. Thanks to typically gorgeous southern California sunshine, weather was never a factor. Why the industry and the state don't work harder to keep more production in California is a mystery to me. The word cover set rarely comes up.

Kristy Winter McCaw does a sensational job as our Production Designer. Another Chapman Grad student. She doesn't have a lot of money to work with, but somehow she makes each location look like a million bucks. She knows the world of the teenager, and remembers how girls will craft their own look on a budget. Every scene in the film is a testament to her hard work.

The dailes look great. One of the benefits of shooting digital. You can screen the day's work at lunch and that night. No waiting for film to return to see if you got the shot. The camera overheats on day 6, one of the failings of the RED. We put a couple of icepacks on the body and don't have any more problems.

The edict by the Orange County school district forbidding us to shoot with summer school students is an issue . Without much of an extras budget, we are hard pressed to make the school look like it was in session. My wife, Annette, and a family friend, Edie Sheppard, became the defacto extra wranglers making phone calls to their OC friends and contacts. Two scenes at the school that could've benefitted from more extras were the scenes with Catharine and Madison's split screen sequence and the cafeteria scene near the end of the picture. For the most part, I think we succeeded.

After the first couple of days, I cut way back on shooting any shots involving real time cellphone and social networking. It worked great in some instances to provide real time tension. But too many hiccups in the connection time were costing us precious time on the set. I decide to schedule a 16th day reserved for shooting all the close-ups, OTS shots and inserts involving technology.

Day two: We lost our restaurant location the previous day. Fortunately, a member of the crew, Rafael Cobos, had worked at a nearby Italian eatery in Anaheim Hills. The restaurant is Foscari Italian cuisine, and the owner agrees to let us shoot there. It's a charming location, but we can't start shooting until 7A and we've got a hard out at 10A. We're shooting the dinner scene where Debbie discovers the sexting photos. I throw out the shot list and decide to shoot the scene in one long dolly shot. We nail it on the fourth take.

The second day is tough because it involves shooting Madison's suicide scene. Tough to ask an actor to sink to such emotional depths her second day on the set. I walked into makeup an hour before the shot to find Najarra, in black bra and panties with tears streaming down her face, sitting across from Rachel Galey, our fantastic hair and makeup person, applying blood effects to her. She was already in character. I kept our conversation brief not wanting to interrupt her process. I already knew to leave Gayla alone to allow her to get to the place she needed to be with Debbie. We shot the scene where Debbie realizes she's been bullying her own daughter right before that. Gayla gave me exactly what I was looking for in terms of the emotional shock the scene requires. After that, I had no doubts she would kick it up a notch when she discovers Madison in the tub.

Shooting in a practical bathroom can be difficult due to the lack of space. Even more so when the emotional content of the scene is so high. Kristi found a great shower curtain that Soren immediately capitalized on. He shot through it to produce the effect of a many-fractured Debbie as she discovers her daughter. Another example of a great crew thinking outside the box.

Jocelyn R.C., the second AC, and Chad Tomlinson, the sound mixer help keep things light on the set. Their great sense of humor and high energy help during dead time on set. It's also Jocelyn whose character closes out the peer counseling scene on a humorous note.

The school scenes go off as well as could be expected given the problems we ran into with extras. Additionally, you're always limited when working with minors on a set in terms of shooting time.

The steadicam sequences of Catharine and Madison crossing the school quad towards a point of near collision took time to rehearse. We used a steadicam for those shots and a number of 2nd A.D.s to handle crowd control across a busy campus.

Shooting the cafeteria scene also required a lot of staging. I had scripted another lengthy tracking sequence patterned after like movement in Van Sant's "Elephant." The purpose was to connect the activity of the students to convey a sense of the random ways in which they interact and disconnect from one another.

The one night shoot was at a supermarket in Huntington Beach. We find a Grocery Outlet that let us shoot after hours. We ran into problems, however, when we were unable to turn off the store's "ATTENTION SHOPPERS" intercom messages broadcasting special bargains. The employee on duty could not find the kill switch, so we ended up shooting takes between the 10-minute intervals between messages.

In keeping with the realistic tone of the film, I wanted to track the Debbie character through the store until she runs into Beth. Instead of using a conventional dolly, we propped Soren up on a standard refrigerator dolly and wheeled him behind Debbie as she shopped. We ended up with a shot that looks more realistic than if we had laid down tracks for a Fisher-dolly.

Soren's staging and camerawork is outstanding. The setups are efficient, lean, creative. I spent eight years in an editorial capacity at Disney Studios watching rushes from all of their features. The operative word at any studio is coverage. And why not? When you're spending millions of dollars you have the luxury of covering every angle, every actor. We have no such luxuries. But I know what I need having worked it out on paper. And talent is delivering.

The second week begins with Jana and Michael nailing down Mike Kelly for the part of Jacob and James Maslow for the role of Brandon. Our principal cast is now complete. Mike has a guy next-door quality to him, exactly what I'm looking for in the part. When I rehearse with him, I tell him Jacob isn't a bad kid. He's only looking to put some cash in his pocket when he takes the job with Debbie. What starts out as a favor for his boss ends up spiraling out of control. Gradually, his conscience will override his wallet. I have to tell him to lay off the weights during shooting; he has bulging biceps and I don't want him looking too manly. I also need him to work on his skateboarding for a couple of scenes.

James looks like a modern day Romeo, a real heartthrob type. He has recently been cast as one of the leads for Nickelodeon's new series "Big Time Rush." He's a very calm, centered young man. He's focused on his career and comes across as philosophical away from the set. He appears to have a very bright future ahead of him. In a sense, his is the toughest role in the film. He's an imaginary character. An illusory visual creation of Catharine's fantasy mouthed by Debbie's dialogue. It's a difficult balancing act, but he pulls it off effortlessly.

Ben Peake, Billy's younger brother, designs a fun and cost effective video game for use in the scene at Jacob's house. It works great. I end up casting my eight year old son, Donovan, to play Jacob's younger brother, Ben, named for Billy. Soren and Mike Kelly have a good rapport with Donovan and help him pull off the scene like a pro.

The third week is scheduled to shoot at and around my house. I'm breaking the cardinal rule of never letting a film crew in your own house, but will make it easier days for the crew. They can wrap soft, meaning leave the equipment locked up in my house, with the truck parked right outside. Thankfully, my wife gives her blessing.

Several of the crew decide to crash at my place during the week to avoid any commute time.

The toughest part of shooting at my house is that it serves as Catharine's home. I'll be recreating the self-mutilating scenes in the bedroom and bathroom where my own daughter cut. Great for realism, bad for the psyche. I have to block it out, but my wife stays away during those days. I remind myself we're making this film to start a dialogue about the subject matter. The scenes call for a certain level of detachment from the character due to the nature of self-injury. But Lily's a pro and nails it.

The soccer scene turned out better than expected. Jane Mitsumori, a wonderful physical therapist who treated me after a car accident, is a soccer mom's mom. Her daughter is a club player and she recruits the girls from the league to field the teams in the script. One concern: Najarra has never played soccer. I shift her to goalie and turn her over to Jane's girls. They work patiently with her at one end of the field, while I choreograph the game movement at the other. Soren shoots the game scenes holding the RED camera on his shoulder while running/tracking the action of the ball movement through the moving maze of players. In this instance, it really helps to have an athletic DP. Later, we run into a problem when Najarra is playing goalie and is supposed to allow a shot to go by her. She's so into character as a goalie, she intuitively blocks several shots. Problem is, we're running out of daylight. It's tough because I want the shot to look like it's part of a real game. Finally, she dives at a ball just beyond her reach and collides with the ground defeated. We get the shot and move on. One more day of shooting remains. In the shots of the spectators at the soccer game, you can see my daughters Genevieve and Celeste alongside their big sister, Aida, who is the basis for the lead character of Catharine.

The last day, like many shoots, feels anticlimactic. Everyone's tired and you always wrap too late to party. But this is a tight group and we're all aware of what we accomplished in a short period of time. A film crew becomes like a family, though a dysfunctional one to be sure. We will have three wrap parties over the next two weeks to cement our shared feature.

I cannot say enough about the herculean efforts of my Producer, Jana Winternitz. Getting a feature film from prep through production in less than 3 months time is amazing, but ridiculously so when you consider it was her first time. I felt so comfortable with the job she did, I never hesitated to spend more money when the shoot dictated it. She worked diligently behind the scenes to keep everything running smoothly, making it possible for me to concentrate on directing.

Billy Peake deserves considerable recognition for functioning in several capacities on the shoot, especially in pre-production.

Every crew member deserves my highest praise. Special thanks to Cory Reeder, Amber Dubeshter, Eric Ulbrich, Dillon Morris, Ron Drynan and Emanuele Parini.

POST PRODUCTION

I'm in the midst of post shoot depression. As grueling as shooting a film is, there's nothing else like it in the world. It takes awhile for me to return to the routine of normalcy. But the work never stops. The process of editing is tedious, viewing and assembling hours of footage. My editor, Zach Anderson, is working overtime to get a rough cut to me in 2 weeks. We're trying to meet the deadlines for submission to the Sundance and Slamdance Film Festivals. I'm practically living with Zach during the first cut; he takes my notes and runs with them.

Zach knows what I want: a cut that delivers just enough information from frame to frame and scene to scene to keep the viewer engaged. I want simply to tell the story, let the audience participate in the narrative and, hopefully, be surprised. He doesn't disappoint. His painstaking work results in a cut that doesn't call attention to the edit, but remains seamless in telling the story. He also puts together a genius temp dub. Within a week of the rough cut, we've made substantial trims and even shuffled the order of some scenes. We haven't even begun the sound, ADR and scoring but end up submitting to Slamdance on the last day.

While we're waiting to hear, Zach and I fine tune with the help of our DIT, Tashi Trieu. Zach had worked with him in the past and recommended him highly. Tashi is a fantastic colorist, a master with the Autodesk Smoke and Flame programs. He's also a talented DP in his own right. He has proved invaluable to me in nearly every aspect of the postproduction process up through the point of sale.

Mike Robertson, also recommended by Zach, is brought on to handle sound. Sound has a huge effect on the audience's attention. The aspects of dialogue, ADR, ambient sound, silence and music must all work together in rhythm to manipulate the audience's emotions to engage with the characters, the story. Mike's a real pro and gives me 24/7 effort.

November 23, 2009

We get word that the film has been accepted to Slamdance, the world's premier indie film festival. It has the indie film feel that Sundance used to have before it became the equivalent of a mini-studio system. All the hard work has paid off.

December, 2009

Zach and Mike are still refining picture and sound. Now to address the score. Zach had been using a track from the "Gone Baby Gone" soundtrack by an artist named Lisbeth Scott. Her amazing talents can be heard on several of the biggest movies of the last few years, "Avatar,"

"Sherlock Holmes," "Iron Man2," in addition to the HBO series "True Blood." I contact the record company to inquire about the rights to the music, but it's Disney owned and a no go. With nothing to lose, I track down Lisbeth online and ask if she can be of any help in acquiring the music. She emails me later that night and asks for a copy of the film, promising to watch and respond when she gets back from out of town.

Three days pass. Lisbeth calls me. She loved the movie so much she wants to score it. I'm tongue tied for a moment, but have the sense to say "yes." She cuts me a great deal and begins to work on it almost immediately.

Lisbeth's complete score is perfect, better than I could've ever imagined. It's incredibly moving and has the added effect of enriching the performance on the screen. She also turns out to be one of the nicest people I have ever met.

One of the last credits I add...

This is a film by everyone who worked on it.

I hate the "film by" credit that most directors take. It's an insult to screenwriters, where the idea and story begin. With the exception of true auteurs like Woody Allen, John Sayles, and Spike Lee who write, direct, produce, and act in their film, I wish Hollywood would do away with it. Film is collaborative; I couldn't have made "@urFRENZ" without the help and input of all my crew.

We finish a day before we leave for Slamdance. 7 months from script to Park City. Not bad. I tell my crew awards are nice, but we've already won.

THE FESTIVAL AND THEREAFTER.

(or, I just came back from Sundance, now what?)

The Slamdance/Sundance Film Festival in 2010 was a dream come true. I was showcasing my film in Park City, Utah, the recognized center of the universe of independent film. If you're a filmmaker, this is your Mecca. Pack and dress for the snow. Slamdance is headquartered in historic Park City at the Treasure Mountain Inn, while across town is Sundance.

In the two-month run-up to Park City, my manager's phone was ringing off the hook. Agencies, Production companies, and buyers, were all interested in me, my film. It was nice to be pursued. The possibilities were endless. Sales Agents approach us to shop our film at the festival. Some will shop us for nothing down, others want us to pay them an upfront fee, anywhere from 3-5K. We find one agency we like, but they demand that we hire a publicist that they're comfortable with. There are any number of high profile parties and industry sponsored events during the week. A good publicist can get you on the invite lists, and the red carpets for photo ops to raise visibility. They typically cost about 4K per month and often require you hire them for a minimum of 2-3 months. But when their publicist declines due to a lack of time, the sales agency decides they're not interested. Before the festival, Monique Moss, of Integrated PR, cuts us a great deal and we hire her to help us promote the film.

FLASH FORWARD

January 21-28, 2010. The Slamdance Film Festival. Next to being on set, this was the best time of my indie filmmaker life. A celebration of the art of film, unsullied by the business side. A gathering of independent filmmakers enjoying and supporting each other's works. Slamdance's motto is "by Filmmakers for Filmmakers," and they accept only low-budget productions. Their mission is "to nurture, support and showcase truly independent works."

Most of my crew found their way to Park City, which was comforting. It took all of us to get "@urFRENZ" to Slamdance, and it was a good feeling to share in that collaboration. We rent a nice condo down the hill from the center of town. Crew members are welcome to crash and pay what they can.

Through a connection of our Co-Producer, Michael Gallagher, we are offered a chance to premiere our film on youtube, along with a number of films from Sundance. I'm wary of this, concerned that it might affect a potential sale. Within 24 hours, Gravitas Ventures, a preferred aggregator of Warner Bros. Digital Distribution, makes it known in the industry trade Variety, that doing so will put endanger a potential VOD deal in the future. I decide not to put the film on youtube.

CUT TO:

Friday, January 29. We didn't' win any major awards, but we're ecstatic nonetheless. And tired from 8 days of late nights, parties and multiple screenings. (On the flight home, Zach and I come up with an idea for a horror flick. Within a months' time, I will bang out the first draft for the spec, BURN.)

No sooner had I landed at John Wayne Airport in Orange County when I noticed a disquieting lack of sound. The phone has stopped ringing. Without a sale, or a win, the film and I are persona non-grata. I can't get arrested.

In February, we get the following review in Variety. Reprinted with their permission:

Posted: Tue., Feb. 16, 2010, 7:28pm PT
Slamdance
UrFrenz
By JOHN ANDERSON

A Virtually Exposed Prods. presentation. Produced by Jana Winternitz. Executive producers, the Phillips Brothers, Michael and Elaine Gallagher. Co-producer, Michael J. Gallagher. Directed, written by Jeff Phillips.

With: Lily Holleman, Gayla Goehl, Najarra Townsend, Michael Robert Kelly, CaroleAnne Johnson, James Maslow.

Inspired by the Megan Meier cyber-bullying case of 2006, the low-budget, high-reaching "UrFrenz" isn't satisfied to merely dramatize the scandalous MySpace suicide, but uses its various aspects to open a window into Internet abuse, adolescent pathologies and the parental heart of darkness. Briskly paced character play skirts formulaic pitfalls via J. Soren Viuf's creative handheld shooting and remarkable perfs by fledgling thesps Lily Holleman, Najarra Townsend and Michael Robert Kelly. Subject, and a sense of the genuine, could draw a niche aud of teens because they'll recognize their online world, and parents because they fear it.

Helmer Jeff Phillips doesn't spell everything out in his script; he lets the camera do much of the storytelling. Catharine (Holleman) virtually runs off the screen in the opening shots -- she's been running for awhile, it seems, and from herself. When she changes in front of a mirror, we see old, self-inflicted scars on her stomach, and fresher lacerations on her thighs.

Catharine is a "cutter," and the cause, at least partly, seems to be her abandonment by her childhood pal Madison (Townsend). Resentment over being unfriended in real life explains why Catharine thoughtlessly passes along a nasty rumor about Madison and her boyfriend. Very little, however, explains the reaction of Madison's mother, Debbie (Gayla Goehl), who slowly, but with increasingly venomous intent, uses a phony online personality named Brandon (played in Catharine's fantasies by James Maslow) on a fictional site called UrFrenz to seduce the lonely, insecure and self-destructive girl. Where Debbie plans to take all this scheming isn't clear at first, even to her, but imminent catastrophe seems to loom over every chatroom exchange.

Phillips doesn't in fact give viewers what they expect, but he does deliver a perfectly plausible scenario for what, even in real life, was an unbelievable narrative. Debbie, having turned she-bear over the perceived abuse of her daughter by Catharine, has had the good fortune to hire high school senior Jacob (Kelly) as her real-estate-office gofer. Jacob becomes Debbie's online guide to chatrooms and Web jargon, and while it isn't quite clear what the otherwise decent guy thinks he's doing -- Debbie's clearly not up to anything good -- the tutorials he provides his boss in online culture also serve as a primer for auds unfamiliar with the language of social networking.

But what makes "UrFrenz" really special isn't educational, but emotional: The waifish, underfed Catharine is oftentimes the picture of teen misery, and young Holleman makes her not just sympathetic but iconic. While Townsend and Kelly naturally capture the unpleasant attitudes of self-entitled teens, Holleman gives us the high-wire hormonal fragility of the unpopular teenage girl. All three should benefit largely from the showcase of "UrFrenz."

Tech credits are generally good, and Lisbeth Scott's score is perfection.

That review is enough to buoy my spirits for months. The goal remains: get the film a mainstream theatrical release.

"@urFRENZ" continues to rack up accolades on the festival circuit. In March of 2010, we play at California's Method Film Festival, which spotlights actors. We're up against stiff competition from name talent like Laura Linney, Steve Buscemi, and Brian Cox. To my great joy and surprise, we dominate the festival. Lily Holleman wins the event's Christie Geraldine Page Award for Best Actress, while Najarra Townsend takes home Best Supporting Actress. "@urFrenz," wins the prize for best feature at the festival.

I couldn't be happier for my talent. A brief word on them:

Lily Holleman was everything I was looking for in the role and so much more. I can't imagine anyone else as Catharine. She kept finding uncharted nuances in the role on the page that increased the onscreen vulnerability of the character and strengthened the emotional connection to the audience. You can't ask for more of your talent.

Najarra Townsend descended into melancholy so completely she deserves a medal for courage. She kept the biggest secret in the script and played it close to the vest. When the reality of her situation becomes clear to us, we are amazed at her ability to maintain focus as the life was slowly unraveling from her character.

Gayle Goehl is my hero. She portrays the mother you love to hate so convincingly that during Slamdance people on the streets of Park City, Utah would approach and tell her, "you're such a great bitch." She is a force and challenged me to be a better director. I learned a great deal from watching her prepare for the role. The fierce determination of her character is enough to make you forget she's one of the sweetest people you will ever meet.

CaroleAnne Johnson was the first person we cast. As the role of Catharine is rooted in my own daughter, Aida, the role of Beth is based on my wife, Annette. (The curly blond hair alone is enough to make them look like sisters.) CaroleAnne is a quiet fighter in the role and admirably portrays every parent who must walk the fine line between parenting a teen and respecting their growth as individuals.

Michael Robert Kelly and James Maslow. Wow. The yin and yang of the average boy next door and the epitome of the male fantasy. The soul of the woman is at stake in this film; Jacob is the bait and Brandon the trap. Between the two of them, they complement the archetypes so thoroughly, that only later do we realize that beneath the deceptive veneer, lies the conscience and conviction of all that is noble about the human race.

My supporting cast also deserves considerable mention. Among them Bree Essrig, Ryan Kidd, Billy St. John, Charlotte White, Nikki Limo, Vanessa Wolf, and Jana Winternitz, whose acting talents are as brilliant as her head for producing. Thanks to your fantastic performances the film stays on story, never losing its focus. Bravo!

Over the course of the next year, we play at the following festivals: the Awareness Fest, Chesapeake, Flagstaff, Anaheim and Fargo. We nab the Audience Choice award for Best Picture at Awareness. Besides the continued exposure, the best thing about Film Festivals is the chance to meet some terrific filmmakers, and people interested in the preservation of the arts. A short list of sensational folk I've encountered along the way include, Summre Gaston, Dan Mirvish, Laura Klein, Liza Moore, Skye Kelly and Derek Horne. You also get a chance to see the country. Chesapeake, MD, was beautiful. The organizers couldn't have been nicer or more accommodating. Gary Rusen and SARCC in Lebanon, PA, your organization is hugely important in helping to prevent sexual violence. Festivals are also important to the psyche of the independent filmmaker. It's a fact that every artist, from sculptors to musicians, from painters to photographers, works in a business of rejection. Art is subjective. One man's Mona Lisa is another man's Dogs Playing Poker. An artist's motor run on hopes and dreams. Every time we meet with supporters of the arts, our spirits are lifted for weeks to come. To those of you who continue to support and encourage us, words cannot express our gratitude.

Simultaneously…

Word of mouth continues to build for the David Fincher directed film, "The Social Network," which premiered at Sundance the same time our picture was playing at Slamdance. Industry people and champions of our film tell us to hang in there with "@urFRENZ." If the film, which traffics in the same social media world as ours, is a hit, we could coattail their success into renewed interest for our film.

We run off 100 copies of the film, nicely packaged in a DVD case with a cover design. I recommend DISCMAKERS out of New Jersey. They're fast and affordable. Budget roughly $150-200 dollars for this.

My manager shops the film around to every studio and buyer. The subject matter and quality of the film will result in most places taking a good, long look at the film. While the response to the film is enthusiastic across the board, it's not enough to generate a sale. For the same reason every time.

We have no known stars.

Before 2008, the year of the Writer's Guild strike and the collapse of the economy at large in September of that year, independent filmmakers had a much better chance of having their product picked up. But that is no longer the case. Since that time, most of the major studios dropped their independent shingles. Fox Searchlight and Sony Pictures Classics are all that remains. Studios will by and large not commit to spending millions of dollars on a marketing campaign without known talent. That definition is specious, in and of itself. Apart from A-list talent like a Will Smith or Brad Pitt, what constitutes a name for one buyer, may not suffice for another. That's including how their foreign sales agents rate the particular talent. One actor might move product in one overseas market, but not another.

With the absence of a true independent distribution system, I'm forced to learn how to self-distribute. Writing the script and making a film is what I'm trained for. Marketing and distribution is a world I know only peripherally. I'm about to get a hard lesson in the new world of independent filmmaking.

We continue to be approached by sales agents. But the reality is, if you have a manager or agent, they can shop the film around just as easily without charging you an upfront fee. I get some good advice from Peter Broderick, a distribution consultant, who wrote the book on self-distribution. He encourages me to consider new strategies for distributing and promoting my film. He tells me the old distribution system is broken. The indie filmmaker does all the work getting the film ready for market, but in selling off the rights to a distributor winds up seeing very little, if any, of the profit.

November 2010. Gravitas contacts us about picking up our film. They are a video-on-demand (VOD) distribution company. They screened "@urFRENZ" and want to license the film. However, they realize that due to the critical and commercial success of "The Social Network," I may want to wait until after Oscar season to get another shot at a theatrical deal. We agree to talk again in April 2011.

In an effort to promote the film, we end up hiring a consultant, who came highly recommended, to raise P&A funds. He sells us on his financial and industry contacts. We strike a deal with him for a flat monthly rate. He wants us to commit to six months, but we settle on three. He now wants to assist in getting a distribution deal and tells us he can get the heads of studios to take his call whereas others can't. He walks the film into Mike Barker, the head of Sony Pictures Classics. While they seriously consider the film, they ultimately pass due to lack of a big name actor. Nine thousand dollars later, I sever relations with him. I'm not happy with the infrequent contact from him that consists mostly of emails hyping the success of other successful indie films in order to buoy my spirits. The hire turns out to be a bust.

May 1st rolls around and still nothing on the theatrical front. We're still in play at a couple of studios, but we're on their schedule to watch the film, make a decision and get back to us. If they call us at all. One of my chief concerns is that we made the first serious film dealing with the issue of cyberbullying. But casting reports appear around town touting films in preproduction dealing with like subject matter make me realize the need to get my film out there. When I read that the ABC Family Channel is premiering an MOW called "Cyberbully," in July, it's settled. I have to get this film out even if it means bypassing a theatrical release.

We contact Gravitas about licensing the film. They're still excited about it and paperwork is exchanged for them to license the film. They want to go to Warner Bros. for a September launch. However, this means I'll need to do additional work in post-production to deliver to the post house they work with. First and foremost is to lock in the existing music.

Originally, the first cut of the film for festivals included commercial music by Jimi Hendrix, She Wants Revenge, and Band of Skulls. They were part of our temp dub, and like many filmmakers, we fell in love with it. After you work on your film for months, you associate it with the music you've chosen. It becomes a problem to dissociate your self from the temp dub. If a studio picks up the film for distribution, they may scrap the dub altogether and replace with music owned by a subsidiary company under the same corporate umbrella.

The music biz is a different animal altogether. You'll likely need an attorney who specializes in that business, as well as a knowledgeable music supervisor. We had hired an independent music supervisor to secure festival rights. In pre-production, people supposedly in the know had told us festival rights can often be had for free. We did not find that to be the case. Our original music supervisor did a good job in securing those rights for a few hundred dollars each. But now we're talking about mainstream distribution for profit, and those rights cost serious money. We can get a low upfront deal, somewhere between a few hundred dollars to a few thousand. But the major music labels want in the neighborhood of 12 cents per download of the film in perpetuity. I'm not a company with an accounting department equipped to handle quarterly download statements. I end up dumping my original music and bringing in a new music supervisor. His name is Greg Sill and he brings with him a long and impressive resume in television and film. He does a fantastic job of finding new songs for the film in a short period of time. Michael Gallagher also comes through for us-again-in finding music for two popular indie bands.

It's crunch time getting the delivery elements ready for Gravitas. I'm indebted to Tashi Trieu, who has assumed post-production supervisor chores. He makes himself available to me nearly around the clock, never overcharges me and delivers on the screen, especially in color correction and Flame. If you look at the dining room sequence where Madison first tells her mother about the rumor, there were lights shining through the dining room curtains in 2 shots. Tashi matched the color and pattern perfectly and corrected the flaws. We go back and clean up some minor picture problems in Smoke and Flame, as well as erasing some audio ticks and pops that get flagged in the QC process. I can't recommend him higher. His contact information is:
Tashi Trieu: www.tashitrieu.com.

In the good old days, pre 2008, filmmakers could negotiate for an upfront fee, a minimum guarantee (MG), and negotiate on the costs of deliverables. Now, MGs are rare and the filmmaker is responsible for all the delivery costs. Independent filmmakers more than likely will be responsible for the following:

ADDITIONAL COSTS TO LOCK PICTURE AND DELIVER:

Music clearance supervisor $500-1000 minimum

Music rights	Free to $3000 and beyond
Picture changes	As needed
Sound remix	As needed
Clearance report	$1000-1500 (you will need this to get your E&O)
Errors & Omission Insurance	$3000-5000 (I recommend purchasing before you begin shooting.)
Close Captioning	$2000
Delivery of elements and Quality Control	$2000

I end up paying for all the above out of pocket. It's gotten to the point where I'm robbing Peter to pay Paul, shifting what little money I have left from one account to another to cover costs. During these times, I remind myself that this is the cost of having the final cut of my film. Only a select few directors get this on major studio pictures. If someone else is controlling the purse strings, you may have to compromise your vision. At the end of the day, I can take solace in the fact that I have not had to sacrifice the artistic merit of my film.

Despite a great deal of interest and several bites, no additional money is forthcoming. In a down economy, money is even scarcer than during normal times for investing in something as speculative as film.

In addition, you'll need to do considerable marketing. We've all read the success stories about films like "Paranormal Activity" and "The Blair Witch Project," films reported to be made for between 15 and 35K. Those were production costs, however. By the time they were released to theatres, the studios that picked them up spent considerable money on marketing costs.

There is a school of thought for independent filmmakers regarding financing. In raising money for the film from investors, set aside 10% for production costs and the other 90% towards marketing. Those percentages sound crazy, but in the new wild west of indie filmmaking, marketing takes precedent. The costs for running promos on network television and cable are very expensive. Print media is also expensive. Thankfully, the digital age makes certain marketing more affordable.

2.0 Website creation	$1000-5000
Website maintenance	$500-800 per month
Digital marketing	$4000-5000 per month minimum

You'll also want to be posting on Facebook, Tweeting and Blogging. I bring on a very creative and hardworking young woman, Traci Hays, who came recommended by Tashi, to oversee my film's digital domain and coordinate all aspects of marketing. She will end up creating our new onesheet (movie poster), the DVD cover, redrafting the press kit and maintaining our website and various links for digital marketing purposes. Jessica Lares returns to convert our existing site, urFRENZmovie.com, to an interactive 2.0 site. It's an enormous amount of work, and so vital in the digital age. Between the two of them, they pull off miracles in the days and weeks leading up to the launch of our film. I am indebted to both of them for their 24/7 efforts in promoting our film. Their contact information is:

Traci Hays: mirage-entertainment.net
Jessica Lares: jessicalares@gmail.com

To get your film in theatres you have two options:

1)   convincing a theatre chain to exhibit the film
2)   renting a theatre, also called fourwalling.

The first option is possible, but the indie filmmaker will be hard pressed to do it without the help of a booking agent. They charge a fee to contact the theatres directly and secure a date and time for display. Major theatre chains may consider you, but you'll need to show them a marketing plan. They want to know you're putting serious money into publicity and advertising costs (P&A). This can run from the low six figures into millions of dollars.

The second option can be done with or without a booking agent. You contact the head of the theatre, who can quote you their costs for renting. A ballpark range can be anywhere between 2000-10K. If you come to an agreement, it's up to you to drive people to see the movie. Again, you need to consider how you will drum up word of mouth for the film.

In August of 2011, Brookwell McNamara Entertainment (BME) showed interest in distributing our film. They are a recognized world leader in producing family programming, and I have worked with them on several feature and television projects. Great guys, and family men, both of them. Sean McNamara and I had gone to film school together at Loyola, and is one of my closest friends. He and his partner David Brookwell, had just produced the hit film, "Soul Surfer," which Sean also directed. Needless to say, I was excited at the chance of partnering with them. They had screened my film early on and loved it, but the time spent getting their own movie ready for market precluded them from working with me earlier on "@urFRENZ." When the deal is concluded, they will acquire the theatrical, foreign, DVD, and TV rights.

Theatre bookings usually take place months in advance. With the VOD premiere set for October 1st, we will be hard pressed to launch a theatrical run for AMPAS and Indie Spirit Awards qualification. (If you have like goals for your own film, you will need to contact those organizations regarding their eligibility requirements.) My manager, Jim Strader, puts me in touch with Greg Rutkowski, a veteran booking agent. We meet in Santa Monica to discuss a limited theatrical run for @urFRENZ. He's a great guy, salt of the earth, who knows all the ins and outs of the exhibition process. Within 3 weeks, he secures a booking at Landmark's Nuart Theatre, one of the best independent cinema theatres in the country. He can be reached at Front RowAttractions.com.

With six weeks remaining until the VOD launch, and less than that for the limited theatrical run, we hire Brigade Marketing out of New York. They will handle all the public relations and interactive marketing for the film. They specialize in digital publicity and social media management.   Traditional print advertising is dead. It's all about maximizing exposure online. I'm excited to see my film released in theatres and on VOD.

The premiere at Raleigh Studios on September 22nd, plays to an overflow crowd and is a success. We also begin to receive some great reviews in the days to come. But it's time to move on.

To the next film.

JP
September 24, 2011

CASTING NOTICE:

TITLE OF FILM: MEAN

FILM SYNOPSIS:
A neo-realist drama set in the backdrop of a Southern California High School. After a nasty rumor is spread, an innocent teenage girl is pushed past her emotional limit. Lost in the world of social networking, a concerned mother walks the fine line of interfering with her daughter's world. The story is driven by the characters and their conflicting objectives.

*MUST BE AVAILABLE FOR SHOOTING DATES: JULY 20TH, 2009-AUGUST 9TH, 2009

DEBBIE KANARD (LEAD), 40's. Real Estate agent and the mother of Madison. She will go to extreme lengths as a mother to protect her teenage daughter. She enters a world she doesn't understand and loses her daughter, her job, her husband and herself in the process. Great dramatic role!

-Looking for females that can play a mother between the ages of 35-45.

CATHARINE PARLEY (LEAD), 16. She is a high school sophomore who is cute, but average in looks. She is self-conscious about her appearance and feels the need to prove herself by putting others down. Strong role for a young actress!

-Looking for females that can play high school of a legal age, between 18-25.

MADISON KANARD (LEAD), 17, is thin and attractive. She is in the midst of female junior woes. She is battling with insecurity and depression. She has a good heart but finds herself entangled and victimized by the harsh world of high school gossip. Great role for an up-and-coming actress!

-Looking for females that can play high school ages 18-25.

-Must be comfortable with very brief, non-sexual, non-gratuitous nudity.

BETH PARLEY (SUPPORTING), is in her late 30's. She is the mother of Catharine and currently experiencing difficulty communicating with her. Beth is a concerned mother but doesn't have the trust of her daughter, thus she is somewhat oblivious.

-Looking for females that can play a mother, ages between 28-39.

JACOB ROSS (SUPPORTING), 17, is a gangly high school boy. He works as Debbie Kanard's assistant in her real estate office. He has a strong moral compass that is tested throughout the film. He must decide between being accepted and doing the right thing.

-Looking for males who can play high school between the ages of 18-25.

BRANDON (SUPPORTING), 17, is good looking with jet-black hair and a winning smile. He is the perfect guy, but only appears in the manifestation of Catharine's daydreams.

-Looking for males between the ages of 18-25.

@urFRENZ

the screenplay

FADE IN OVER CREDITS:

EXT. SANTA ANA RIVERBED - DAY

A young girl of 16, CATHARINE PARLEY, runs through a concrete wash. Clearly distraught, she drops to her knees and utters a primal SCREAM.

INT. CATHARINE'S HOUSE - BATHROOM - DAY

Catharine applies makeup to her face at the mirror. A towel wrapped around her.

Catharine in jeans, wearing a bra, brushes her teeth.

The sound of A HAIR DRYER. She bends over at the waist, her hair flopped over, concealing her face as she BLOW DRIES.

Catharine opens the medicine cabinet door.

INSERT MEDICINE CABINET: Prescription bottles. Her hand grabs one marked "Duloxetine 20 mg. Generic for CYMBALTA."

CLOSE: HER HAND as she shakes out a pill into her palm.

Catharine pops the pill into her mouth and chases with water.

Catharine pulls on a trendy long sleeve tee.

CLOSE-UP:: Her left hand, palm down. She slides on a couple of bracelets and a pink "yes we can" rubber wristband.

CATHARINE'S ARM: for the first time we notice SEVERAL CUTS on her wrist and forearm. We realize she's a self-mutilator. She tugs her sleeve down over them concealing.

INT. SCHOOL - CAFETERIA SERVING ROOM - DAY

Students eat lunch in a modern dining hall.

Catharine stands in line for her food behind other kids at the serving window. She holds her bus tray.

She slides her tray across the metallic surface stopping in front of a FOOD SERVER.

> CATHARINE
> Can I have a juice please?

A plain looking girl in a school sweatshirt walks over. This is HANNAH. Unlike her friend Catharine, she does not appear to be cursed with her own self-awareness.

> HANNAH
> The mystery meat is looking especially
> yummy today.

> CATHARINE
> What to eat?

She selects a PRE-MADE SALAD. Hannah motions the server.

> HANNAH
> Cheeseburger.

> CATHARINE
> I thought you were vegan.

They continue moving down the line stocking their trays with food and drink.

> HANNAH
> I started getting light-headed. My parents
> took me to see a nutritionist.

CATHARINE
You never told me. When?

HANNAH
Two days ago. They did all these blood
tests on me.

CATHARINE
Gross.

HANNAH
Turns out I have an iron deficiency.

INT. SCHOOL - CAFETERIA

Catharine and Hannah walk away from the cashier and into the seating
area. They take a moment to scan the place for the best spot.

CATHARINE
There's a table in the back.

The two walk past several rows of tables. They pass a table full of girls.
The CAMERA LINGERS but only for a second, on an attractive
BRUNETTE. Amidst the talk...

GIRL #1
You think you and Greg will get back
together?

They take their seats at an empty table.

HANNAH
Do you have my Rent CD?

CATHARINE
You need it back?

                         HANNAH
                 We have rehearsal tomorrow.

Catharine's phone RINGTONES go off. She fishes her CELL out of
her pants pocket. She reads the text –

INSERT CELL PHONE SCREEN: BRANDON: Lunch break?

A smile spreads across Catharine's face.

                        CATHARINE
                 It's him.

She TEXTS back mouthing as she does.

                        CATHARINE
                 ...with Hannah.

                         HANNAH
                 You're totally gonna have sex with him
                 aren't you?

                        CATHARINE
                 We're just friends.

                         HANNAH
                 How long has it been?

                        CATHARINE
                 Four weeks tomorrow.

INSERT CELL PHONE SCREEN: BRANDON: Just thinking of
you.

Catharine types back.

                        CATHARINE
                 He's so sweet.

HANNAH
You should buy a black thong for the
occasion.

CATHARINE
Shutup.

HANNAH
You better call me as soon as it happens.

CATHARINE
(sarcastic)
Yeah, I'll call you right when it happens.

Camera RACK FOCUSES across the way on a gangly boy with close cropped hair. JACOB ROSS, is 17 and appears to be taking some interest in Catharine.

INT. CATHARINE'S HOUSE - BEDROOM - NIGHT

The CAMERA LINGERS over Catharine lying asleep in her double-bed. She's facing us, her eyes closed as we TILT UP to show—

The world of a teenage girl. SLOW CIRCLE PAN around the room.

A bookcase displays various mementos accumulated from Catharine's short life. PAN ACROSS a couple of SOCCER TROPHIES for participation.

CONTINUE PANNING to show a family of STUFFED ANIMALS at the base of a wall. Their manufactured expressions of innocence remind us how fragile Catharine's world is. ABOVE IT –

A window is cracked open revealing the night. Continue as –

We PAN across an open CLOSET DOOR. Inside, a dresser with the top drawer out. Colored underthings vie for attention from their like

CLOTHING matches, which hang in bunches from the dowl. Mostly long sleeve tees, jeans.

PAN AROUND to the bedroom door. The BOLT from the top hinge protrudes a good inch and half indicating the door has been removed recently.

CONTINUE PAN. A portable CD STORAGE CASES overflowing with bought and homemade music discs. CONTINUE PANNING TO SHOW –

A desk cluttered with various papers and textbooks.

END PAN back on CATHARINE. She's facing us now, her eyes wide open. Thinking. Wondering. Imagining the possibilities that life holds for her the next day.

INT. SCHOOL - TRIGONOMETRY CLASS - DAY

Catharine takes an exam. At the head of the class, the MATH TEACHER grades papers.

Catharine marks her paper, moves on to the next question which relates to:

INSERT: a problem where TWO CIRCLES INTERSECT.

Catharine looks around her. Not cheating, but grasping at the ether for answers. She returns her focus to the page.

EXT. SCHOOL - ATHLETIC FIELD - DAY

A group of GIRLS run laps around a track for P.E..

Catharine jogs somewhere near the back of the pack. Like most of the others, she looks bored with the inanity of the gym class ritual. We hear a WHISTLE offscreen –

The girls pull up short. Getting their breath, hands on their knees. A FEMALE GYM TEACHER approaches them.

> GYM TEACHER
> Hit the showers ladies.

The girls matriculate inside. Catharine continues to bring up the rear. HOLD ON HER as she walks right past the camera.

INT. SCHOOL - LOCKER ROOM - DAY

LOCKER POV: From inside a long, rectangular gym locker. We don't see Catharine's face, just her upper and lower torso. She sheds her gym top first, a sports bra underneath. She stows it in the locker, exchanging it for her tee shirt.

In the background, we hear some snide chatter directed towards Catharine.

> GIRL (V.O.)
> My Mom says it's Aspergers.

> GIRL #2 (V.O.)
> Whatever it's pronounced, it spells *loser*.

Catharine unties the drawstring holding up her long sweat pants. As they drop to the floor, we notice a number of CUTS on her upper thighs. It's unsettling. She trades the sweats for her jeans. Grabs her notebook and shuts the locker door.

EXT. SUBURBAN STREET - DAY

Catharine rides her bike. We hear a CELL PHONE RINGING.

> CATHARINE (V.O.)
> Hey, if my Mom calls cover for me...
> what do you think?...of course.

EXT. LIBRARY - DAY

To establish.

INT. LIBRARY - COMPUTER WING - DAY

A CLOCK on the wall reads 3:10P.

A row of computers. A cross section of people access them.

Catharine sits TYPING on urFRENZ, a teen social networking site.
We see snippets of the following chat on-line:

INSERT COMPUTER SCREEN: - INTERCUT

CATHARINE: I wish u had a phone.

BRANDON: Tell my Dad to get a job first.

CATHARINE: Whatchu doing right now?

An OLDER MAN sits down at the computer beside Catharine.

BRANDON: Besides thinkin about u?

CATHARINE: :)

EXT. PARK - DAY - CONTINUOUS

A local park. Sunny, verdant. We can still hear the sound of
KEYBOARD CLICKING though much fainter.

> BRANDON (V.O.)
> My parents are freaking out over my sister.

> CATHARINE (V.O.)
> If I was pregnant my Mom would freak out too.

BRANDON (V.O.)
So much for my next suggestion. Kidding!

THE CAMERA RESTS beside a swingset. Catharine swings while...

BRANDON ROUSCH, 17, pushes her from behind. He's good
looking with jet black hair and a winning smile. Looks a little above her
station.

CATHARINE
Tease.

BRANDON
I'm sure she's not that bad.

CATHARINE
Seriously, my Mom would kill me. Or
worse.

BRANDON
What's worse than death.

Beat as we continue PULLING BACK past a large playground set,
climbing toys, swings, etc., set in a sandbox.

CATHARINE
Utah.

Her inflection makes it sound more like a threat, and maybe we
remember that Utah is the capital of long term teen rehab.

BRANDON
I'm gonna enjoy watching my sister get
big and fat.

CATHARINE
Harsh.

                              BRANDON
          She was kind of stuck up when she was
          younger. You know, selfish, the world revolves
          around me type.

                              CATHARINE
          I can relate.

                              BRANDON
          You know someone like that?

                              CATHARINE
          There's this one girl. She's not very nice.

                              BRANDON
          Why do you say that?

The KEYBOARD CLICKING gets louder.

                              CATHARINE (O.S.)
          Cuz' she's a total bitch—

TO THE SOUND OF SOMEONE BACKSPACING 20 TIMES,
THE IMAGE OF CATHARINE SUDDENLY REWINDS
CUTTING OFF HER LAST RESPONSE.

And we realize the above is Catharine imagining the conversation with
Brandon.

INSERT COMPUTER SCREEN: We see an IM "she's a ttl bitch"
backspaced and deleted.

BACK TO SCENE

                              CATHARINE
          She's just not.

                              BRANDON
          Something you wanna tell me?

CATHARINE
We used to be friends. Her family lived
across the street from us.

BRANDON
And...

CATHARINE
And we moved.

Brandon steps away, stops pushing her.

BRANDON
Not what I meant.

CATHARINE
Can we talk about something else?

A beat, as Catherine comes to a stop on the swing.

CATHARINE
Why'd you stop?

BRANDON
You wanna go faster?

Brandon spins her around in her seat, several times, the chains holding
the swing binding with tension above her.

CATHARINE
We should meet.
        (half smiling)
You know, meet. For real.

BRANDON
M I R L. Meet in real life.

CATHARINE
What's wrong?

                              BRANDON
                    What if I'm not what U R expecting?

                             CATHARINE
                    You think I won't like you or something?

                              BRANDON
                          It could happen.

                             CATHARINE
            Never.

HER POV: he lets go the swing and she spins round and round, his
image becoming a blur.

The sound of an electronic JINGLE interrupts the fantasy. Beat and we
see HANNAH appear in the park nearby.

                              HANNAH
                       Are you guys doing it?

INT. LIBRARY - COMPUTER WING - CONTINUOUS

Back at library. Catharine checks her CELL PHONE screen.

"You have one new message from HANNAH 555-7682."

Catharine CLICKS to continue. The message reads:

INSERT CELL PHONE SCREEN: R U GUYZ DOIN IT?

Catharine texts back: GMAB. (Gimme a break)

INSERT CELL PHONE SCREEN: P911 (alternate: parent 911)

Catharine looks to THE CLOCK: It now reads 5:15P.

CATHARINE
Crap.

She returns to the computer. Pecks hurriedly.

CATHARINE: Gotta go.

Catharine LOGS OFF. Grabs her backpack heads for the exit.

CUT TO:

ANGLE ON:

A computer screen. A desktop. <u>And it contains the same conversation between Catharine and Brandon.</u>

We see BRANDON'S urFRENZ page, his familiar PHOTO.

A FEMALE HAND reaches into frame and logs off.

CUT TO:

INT. HOUSE - PARTY - NIGHT

A high school party in progress. Various TEENS drink, dance to MUSIC and socialize. Hannah is there talking to some friends. In the midst of the revelry...

The brunette from the cafeteria scene, MADISON KANARD, 17, thin and hot, chatting with her posse of gals. She looks distracted. Throws down a drink and walks off to the dismay of her friends.

Madison approaches a good looking alpha male, GREG BARNES, who is chatting up another GIRL.

GREG
Hey, Maddy.

MADISON
Greg, can I talk to you?

Greg follows Madison as they exit the living room towards the back bedroom.

CUT TO:

SUPER OVER BLACK - FOUR WEEKS EARLIER

INT./EXT – BETH'S CAR/DRIVEWAY – CATHARINE'S HOUSE - DAY

A two-story stucco home in a suburban tract.

BETH PARLEY, late 30's, slender with pleasant features, sits behind the wheel of a minivan dressed for work. She HONKS the horn.

BETH
(sotto)
Catharine, we're gonna be late.

Beat, Catharine steps out of the house, carrying her backpack. Pulling the front door behind her. She double-checks the lock then heads for the car and climbs in.

Beth backs out of the driveway and into the street.

INT. BETH'S CAR - STREET - DAY

Catharine sits beside her Mom in the passenger seat.

BETH
You get all your homework done?

Catharine MUMBLES something while she ties her shoes.

> BETH

Did you?

> CATHARINE

I said yes.

> BETH

You were mumbling again, I couldn't
hear you.

They ride in silence for a moment.

> BETH

We're having chicken for dinner. Do you
want rice or pasta with it?

> CATHARINE

Rice, I guess.

> BETH

You coming to the airport to pick up
your father?

> CATHARINE

No.

> BETH

He'd like it if you came.

> CATHARINE

Hannah and I are working on our history
report. It's due Friday.

Almost absentmindedly, Catharine looks out the window.

EXT. SCHOOL - DAY

Establish an outdoor southern California High School urban campus. An older school caught between budget cuts and disrepair.

EXT. SCHOOL - QUAD - DAY

Catharine passes the amphitheater as she crosses the quad.

She stops to chat with a group of friends. A long beat and a BELL goes off.

She turns away and heads to class disappearing behind a building. In the background we hear—

>   RANDOM GUY (O.S.)
>   Looking good Maddy.

ANGLE ON:

The top of the amphitheater. Madison wheels a HANDICAPPED STUDENT up an incline.

EXT. SCHOOL - QUAD - DAY

Madison escorts a teenage boy, RICHARD, who suffers from cerebral palsy. He wears a sweater, though it's clearly warm outside.

>   MADISON
>   Time for school Richard. I bet you're glad.

>   RICHARD
>   Yeah.

>   MADISON
>   Me too.

TRACK WITH THEM as Madison wheels him through the quad.

EXT. SCHOOL QUAD - DAY

Madison wheels Richard down a slight incline. We see that she has a natural way with him.

>   MADISON
>   Did you wear that sweater for me?

He blushes.

>   MADISON (CONT'D)
>   I knew it.

>   RICHARD
>   It's my favorite. I got it last Christmas.

>   MADISON
>   I have a couple sweaters at home, but
>   none as nice as that.

She nears Greg and his pals visible in the background.

IN THE BACKGROUND

We FOCUS on Catharine stopping to talk to friends.

She lingers for a beat longer, waves goodbye. She turns away and heads to class. TRACK WITH HER down a hallway –

CONTINUE TRACKING as she turns the corner down another hall.

Beat and coming towards her is Greg Barnes and his crew. Behind them, also coming into frame –

Madison wheels the boy towards a SPECIAL NEEDS ADMIN-
ISTRATOR. (Note: The confluence of Catharine, Madison and Greg
suggests a collision.)

> MADISON
> Hey, Greg.

Greg, barely acknowledges her, walks off with his crew following.

> GREG
> (gestures towards Madison)
> Tell you guys Maddy sucked my cock.

> BUDDY #1
> Dude, serious?

> GREG
> Webber's party. In his sisters' room.

> BUDDY #2
> Where the hell was I?

> GREG
> Pro'lly getting your ass kicked at beer pong.

The others LAUGH in approval. Coming into focus—

CATHARINE walks past the group of boys unnoticed.

More LAUGHTER in the background. But our attention is with—

CATHARINE, who has overheard them. As she turns the corner—

She sees Madison in the b.g., regarding Greg.

Catharine continues heading to class.

INT. SCHOOL - CLASSROOM - DAY

Catharine sits in the row second from the last trying her best to look inconspicuous. At the head of the class—

The teacher, MR. ESDALE, tall, bespectacled, lectures.

THE BLACKBOARD contains notes on Bram Stoker's classic text, *Dracula*. One stands out: <u>a vampire must be invited in</u>.

                         ESDALE
               We left off with the reading of The
               Westminster Gazette, page 188 in the
               text. A child encounters the Bloofer Lady
               and is found emaciated with two tiny holes
               in his neck.

Catharine looks out across the sea of students.

                         ESDALE
               This is an example of Dracula as a mass
               media agent. You encounter him, you are a
               celebrity. Who can tell me what forms of
               mass media Stoker employs?

The class is nonresponsive. A CHUNKY KID raises his hand.

                         CHUNKY KID
               The telegraph.

                         ESDALE
               Good, what else? Angela.

He indicates a girl, ANGELA, sitting in the middle of class.

                         ANGELA
               I don't know. The girl, Mina's diary?

                              ESDALE
                I'm looking for something a little more
                public.
                              (beat)
                In the handout you were given, the author
                talks about the Count as a kind of paparazzi.

A HISPANIC BOY speaks up. Other STUDENTS chime in.

                          HISPANIC BOY
                You mean like the dudes that killed Princess Di.

                              ANGELA
                They're such assholes.

                              ESDALE
                Alright, alright. Madison, did you read
                the article?

Madison looks up from flipping through another book, HAMLET. She
straightens up a little in her seat.

                             MADISON
                Yeah. She mentions the newspaper
                ty-pog...typo-graphy. And Seward's phono-
                graph diary.

                              ESDALE
                On wax cylinder. Excellent. So the author
                uses various technology from recording,
                transcription, the telegraph and newspaper,
                all modern communication tools of the time
                to enforce his point.

Catharine begins TEXTING on her phone.

INSERT CELL PHONE SCREEN: Didja hear about Madison?

CLOSE TEXT SCREEN: "I heard she gave Greg a blowjob at the party."

TILT TO SHOW – a female classmate, ZOE, giggles at the text on her phone. RACK FOCUS as she looks across the class to Catharine, who nods.

BACK TO SCENE

> ANGELA
> So, does that mean people were getting
> bit on purpose to become famous?

> ESDALE
> No, but it's worth noting that the bite
> of a vampire made you an instant media
> sensation.

> STUDENT
> You could tweet, "hey guys, guess who
> just bit me?"

INT. SCHOOL - HALLWAY - DAY

An open locker displays the things that define a high school girl. A PHOTO COLLAGE of cute boys and boy bands clipped from teen magazines. Stickers of small furry animals, ironic sayings, and bright colors surround a small MIRROR. Through it's reflection we see...

Catharine. She shuts her locker door.

> HANNAH (O.S.)
> Cath.

Hannah walks over.

> CATHARINE
> How was the party?

HANNAH
Okay. Sorry you didn't get invited.
(Catharine shrugs)
You should've seen Steve Samuels. He was
all over Julie Michaels.

CATHARINE
The freshman girl?

BEGIN TRACKING with Catharine and Hannah as they navigate the
crowded hallways, flanked by lockers on either side.

HANNAH
He was just doing it to rub it in Emily's face.

CATHARINE
How pathetic.

HANNAH
Tell me about it. They only broke up
like three weeks ago.

Around her, STUDENTS cram food, energy drinks and chat between
classes, all the while TEXTING, TWEETING and CALLING.

INSERT VARIOUS CELL PHONE SCREENS:

Text snippets and downloads of e-chat. The daily minutiae that takes
precedence over grades, exams and papers to write.

HANNAH
He's just using her—

The girls reach the end of the hallway.

HANNAH
Wanna do something?

CATHARINE
Can't. My mom's totally on my ass about
grades.

HANNAH
'Kay, call me later.

Catharine pushes through the double doors and exits.

EXT. BUSINESS PARK - DAY

A pleasant business park in a manufactured natural setting.

INT. REAL ESTATE OFFICE - DAY

The office frames a series of desks and computer workstations. A
PLACARD reads: Debbie Kanard Realty.

Jacob who we saw briefly in the cafeteria, sits across from Debbie who
reviews his APPLICATION.

DEBBIE
(reading)
So you moved here when you were ten?

A DOOR opens behind them.

MADISON (O.S.)
Mom, I'm dropping off my books on the
way to soccer practice—

Madison enters dressed for soccer.

MADISON
Sorry.

> DEBBIE
> Do you know my daughter, Madison?
>   (beat)
> This is Jacob, he's going to be working
> part time for me.

> MADISON
> Were you in my tenth grade bio class?

> JACOB
> Mariano's. Yeah, I think so.

> DEBBIE
> You need a ride to the game?

> MADISON
> Thanks, but I have to stop at a friend's
> house first.

Madison exits, pulls the door shut behind door.

> DEBBIE
> Tell me about yourself.

> JACOB
> Like what?

> DEBBIE
> What you do when you're not in school?

> JACOB
> Play guitar a little. I'm sort of in a band.

INT. JACOB'S HOUSE - GARAGE - INTERCUT

JUMPCUTS: Jacob tooling around with his guitar at home.

BACK TO SCENE

                          DEBBIE
What about sports?

                          JACOB
Not really.

                          DEBBIE
Says on your application you're a
senior. You ever think about college
or learning a trade?

                          JACOB
Maybe. I think about it. Right now I just
need to make bank, you know.

                          DEBBIE
Okay. Well, the job consists mostly of
helping me market my business. I'm a real
estate broker as you know. I'm responsible
for ensuring the transaction of buying and
selling a home is completed properly. I share
the office with another broker, Sharon.
You'll meet her.

Jacob nods, he gets it.

                          DEBBIE
How successful I am depends on my ability
to generate new business. I do that through
referrals, advertising listed properties, open
houses and networking.

EXT. SUBURBAN STREET - DAY - INTERCUT

JUMPCUTS: Debbie working the neighborhood. Talking to people,
showing homes.

BACK TO SCENE

>   DEBBIE
>   Referrals and word-of-mouth is where I
>   generate eighty five percent of business.
>   Do you have any idea why that is?

>   JACOB
>   (beat; a little unsure)
>   Because the more people like you, the more
>   they want to work with you.

>   DEBBIE
>   Yeah. Something like that. The home is
>   the most important symbol of the American
>   family. It also tends to be their primary
>   investment. Which means they need to trust
>   me if I'm going to do business with them.

Jacob nods.

>   DEBBIE
>   In a very real sense, I'm not just selling
>   homes. I'm selling myself.

THE WINDOW: Pages of several property listings in the area.

>   CUT TO:

EXT. SCHOOL - PARKING LOT - DAY - INTERCUT FLASH
FORWARD

Jacob talks to Madison outside the parking lot. They stand close to each
other holding their cell phones transmitting infrared wireless.

Madison says something to Jacob, one word, but we can't tell what she
says.

DEBBIE (O.S.)
Here's what you'll be delivering.

BACK TO SCENE

Debbie indicates STACKS OF BOXES are propped up against the far wall. Beside them are real estate yard signs, riders, lock boxes, key boxes, and brochure boxes.

DEBBIE
These are calendars.

She lifts the flap on an open box. Produces a CALENDAR featuring her name and business info at the top.

DEBBIE
You'll also be handing out newsletters, notepads, fliers—

JACOB
Cool.

DEBBIE
Refrigerator magnets are smart, practical, and most importantly, permanent. People hold onto these for years.

Jacob picks up a FLIER. Reads.

JACOB
DebbieKanardHomes dot com.

DEBBIE
That's my website. But you won't have to worry about that.
          (beat)
Now on Sunday afternoons at five o'clock or so, you'll need to collect the open house signs

DEBBIE (CONT)
and drop them off at the office. You have a
car, right?

JACOB
Yeah, a Civic. It's got a hatchback.

DEBBIE
Perfect.

Jacob scans a NEWSLETTER filled with real estate information.

JACOB
What do I do if someone asks me
questions?

DEBBIE
Be personable, polite. Have them call me
directly. Try to smile a little.

Jacob nods, then spots a FOR SALE SIGN with Debbie's picture on it.
She notices Jacob holding back a smile.

DEBBIE
What's so funny?

JACOB
Nothing, it's just...
(beat)
We have this neighbor who sells homes, and
her face is on the bus stop over on Adams.
But it doesn't look anything like her. It's like
a twenty year old picture.

DEBBIE
That's Grace Kellogg. She was a local
beauty queen back in high school. That's
how people remember her.

And if we've listened closely, maybe we catch just a trace of bitterness in her tone.

> JACOB
> Isn't that, like cheating?

> DEBBIE
> First impressions count for a lot. If people
> see a beautiful face on a bus stop, they
> project that image when they meet her.

> JACOB
> I guess.

Subconsciously, she quickly primps her hair.

> DEBBIE
> Hopefully, my clients will see the person
> beneath the surface.

INT. KANARD HOUSE - FRONT ROOM - DAY

Debbie enters with daughter CASEY, 7. TRACK WITH THEM into –

LIVING ROOM

Casey makes for the sofa, remotes the TV on. While Debbie opens the rear door to let some air in, continues to the kitchen to turn her coffee pot on. She CONTINUES into the –

DINING ROOM

Where she sets her mail down on the table, sorting it.

In the background, a door OPENS/CLOSES. Someone enters.

> DEBBIE
> Maddy?

Debbie sees –

FRONT ROOM

Madison dumping her backpack, before hurrying upstairs.

> DEBBIE
> I thought you had peer counseling.
> (off her silence)
> Something the matter?

> MADISON (O.S.)
> I'm fine.

Debbie moves to the stairs. Her POV as Madison disappears in the upstairs hallway. Beat and we hear a door SLAM.

INT. KANARD HOUSE - STAIRS - DAY

Debbie ascends the stairs...

INT. KANARD HOUSE - UPSTAIRS HALLWAY - DAY

Debbie turns down the hall and stops outside a door. She looks about to knock when –

She hears her daughter's CELL ring.

> MADISON (O.S.)
> Hey....pissed. You heard what Catharine
> Parley told Zoe? What a bitch...I know, I
> can't believe I was ever friends with her.

Debbie REACTS, concerned. Continues hovering for a beat.

EXT. KANARD HOUSE - NIGHT

To establish a two-story single-family home.

INT. KANARD HOUSE - DINING ROOM - NIGHT

Dinner. Debbie passes a salad bowl over to her husband, TERRY. Maddy sits across from them eating in relative silence, across from Casey.

> TERRY
> You know the Howards are getting
> divorced?

> DEBBIE
> You're kidding?

> TERRY
> He just walked into the living room, told
> her he'd met someone else and that was that.

Debbie notices Madison isn't talking too much.

> DEBBIE
> Maddy, you're awfully quiet.

> TERRY
> School okay? How's Brianna doing? Haven't
> seen her in awhile.

Madison shrugs.

> DEBBIE
> I was cleaning out the office earlier and I
> came across some old photos from your
> soccer team two years ago. You ever talk
> to any of those girls—

Madison SLAMS her fork down.

> MADISON
> Real subtle, Mom.

> DEBBIE
> You stomped upstairs and I went to see
> what was the matter. What's up with
> you and Catharine?

> CASEY
> I want some more milk.

> MADISON
> Great, now you're spying on me—

> DEBBIE
> Please.

> CASEY
> I want some more milk please.

> DEBBIE
> In the fridge.

Casey takes her cup and disappears into the kitchen.

> DEBBIE
> What happened?

> TERRY
> The Parley's girl? I haven't seen them
> since they moved.

> DEBBIE
> I run into Beth now and then.

Madison doesn't react. Her silence confirming.

TERRY
Honey, your mother asked you a question.

Madison drops her fork for emphasis.

MADISON
Look, it's not that big a deal. She started
a rumor.

DEBBIE
What did she say?

MADISON
I don't know. Mean stuff.

DEBBIE
What kind of mean stuff?

MADISON
(beat)
Promise you won't freak out.

DEBBIE
I can't promise I won't be upset, but I
promise not to yell.

MADISON
She said I went down on this guy.

DEBBIE
What?!

Debbie tenses. She looks to Terry, who wears a different expression of
distaste. Debbie checks him with a look as Casey walks back in.

DEBBIE
Why would someone say that about
anyone?

CASEY
What'd who say?

TERRY
Nothing, Casey. Drink your milk.

MADISON
Cuz she's a little...
            (spelling it out)
B I T C H.

DEBBIE
You have every right to be angry. I'm
angry.

MADISON
I'll handle it.

DEBBIE
Maybe I should call Beth—

MADISON
No. You promised me you wouldn't
freak out.

DEBBIE
How is that freaking out?

MADISON
This, this is freaking out.

DEBBIE
I think she should know that her daughter
is saying hurtful things.

MADISON
            (upset)
You'll just be making it worse.

She pushes her chair away from the table, getting to her feet.

MADISON
I'm going to my room.

She walks out. Terry looks to Debbie, shakes his head.

INT. KANARD HOUSE - HOME OFFICE - NIGHT

Debbie is sitting at her computer logging onto urFRENZ. The minute she does, the program asks for her PASSWORD and USER NAME. She enters the information and...

INSERT COMPUTER SCREEN: MADISON'S WALL. She's successfully logged on to her daughter's page. The familiar "hello" is the first thing we see. On it –

We see PHOTOS of Madison and some of her friends. There are STILLS of some of her favorite bands, books, and movies. A photo of MADISON and GREG BARNES looking cozy suggests their former relationship. If we don't look too closely, we might think we're on Catharine's page, their interests being similar. And maybe we can understand the basis of a former friendship.

INSERT COMPUTER SCREEN: She clicks on Profile and scrolls on the Comments page. Not much there.

Debbie hits paydirt when she clicks over to the...

INSERT COMPUTER SCREENS: IM SECTION. A STRING of instant angry messages from an earlier conversation is posted.

MADISON: Cuz she's a loser. Hear that world? Catharine Parley is a NOSY BITCH!!!!

Debbie leans back in her seat to digest this information. She looks concerned about the content, her daughter. Beat and...

A DROP OF WATER strikes the table. She looks up to see...

A WATER STAIN the size of a fist, on the ceiling. Debbie reacts with exhausted frustration.

INT. REAL ESTATE OFFICE - DAY

INSERT: a check to Jacob in the amount of fifty dollars.

Debbie signs the check and hands it over to Jacob who stands beside her holding his SKATEBOARD.

> DEBBIE
> Don't forget about picking up the signs
> Sunday at 5. You have the office key,
> right?

Jacob produces his KEY RING, indicating. He starts to walk away when —

> DEBBIE
> Jacob, how well do you know computers?

> JACOB
> Pretty well, why?

> DEBBIE
> Do you know anything about urFRENZ?

> JACOB
> What do you want to know?

> DEBBIE
> I need to create a whattyacallit, a profile.
> Can you show me how?

Jacob turns and moves behind her. He types in urFRENZ on the web page.

Beat and the urFRENZ HOME PAGE APPEARS on screen.

> JACOB
> It's pretty simple.

> DEBBIE
> I'm afraid a lot of the internet still
> intimidates me.

> JACOB
> No worries. Type in your name...

He begins to type in her name, Debbie Kanard.

> JACOB
> Now it'll ask you a bunch of questions
> about yourself. Interests, school, stuff
> like that.

> DEBBIE
> What...what if I don't want to use my name?

> JACOB
> Whose name do you want to use?

> DEBBIE
> I don't know, make one up.

> JACOB
> (beat)
> Lemme guess, your daughter has an
> account and you want to spy on her?
> (off Debbie's look)
> All parents do it. That's why most kids
> have multiple accounts.

>   DEBBIE
>   Actually, it's not *my* daughter I want to
>   spy on.

Jacob looks confused.

>   DEBBIE
>   There's a girl who's been spreading
>   vicious rumors about Maddy at school.

>   JACOB
>   Maybe I know her. What's her name?

>   DEBBIE
>   Catharine Parley. She's a sophomore.

>   JACOB
>   Nah.

>   DEBBIE
>   I want to find out what she's been saying
>   about her.

>   JACOB
>   What did your daughter say?

>   DEBBIE
>   (hiding embarrassment)
>   Basically, she called her a slut.

>   JACOB
>   Girls do that.
>   (beat)
>   So...you want to get on to this other girl's
>   site and what?

>   DEBBIE
>   Talk to her. Gain her confidence.

> JACOB
> You mean mess with her.

> DEBBIE
> No...I'm just trying to protect my daughter.
> (beat)
> Will you help me?

> JACOB
> (beat; shrug)
> You're the boss.

MONTAGE

Shots to show Debbie and Jacob creating a fake profile.

-A boy's name is entered. BRANDON ROUSCH, age 17.

-A PHOTO of a good-looking TEEN BOY is pulled off another internet site and pasted onto Brandon's page.

-They choose a PUBLIC PROFILE (important)

-Rounding out the boy's profile are his music tastes (metal), his interests (first person shooter video games), skateboarding and hanging out.

> DEBBIE (O.S.)
> Jacob. It's important that you don't tell
> Madison about this. She'll just get mad.

LATER -

Jacob sits alongside Debbie at the keyboard.

> JACOB
> First, you're going to need to make a friend
> request. Click on that field.

Debbie clicks on the REQUEST field.

> DEBBIE
> What now?

> JACOB
> (indicating)
> It says she's online.

INT. CATHARINE'S HOUSE - BEDROOM - INTERCUT AS NEEDED

Catharine is tooling around on her urFRENZ page. A SOUNDBEEP alerts her to click to FRIEND REQUESTS. She sees —

A picture of BRANDON showing who the message is FROM and a message that says Brandon wants to be your friend. Intrigued perhaps by his good looks, Catharine clicks the APPROVE box.

> JACOB (O.S.)
> Sweet, we're in.

INSERT COMPUTER SCREEN: BRANDON: Heyyy.

> DEBBIE (V.O.)
> What do I say?

> JACOB (V.O.)
> Just talk to her?

CATHARINE: Hi. Who is this?

> JACOB (V.O.)
> Tell her the PSA link.

INSERT COMPUTER SCREEN: her link to a local rock band, PSA.

BRANDON: Your link on PSA.

CATHARINE: You like them?

> JACOB (V.O.)
> I'll answer this.

BRANDON: I saw 'em at Hoagie's. The bass guitarist shreds.

CATHARINE: I saw them six months ago. They rocked!

CATHARINE: U go to Western?

> JACOB (V.O.)
> Your call.

> DEBBIE (V.O.)
> I don't know...home schooled.

BRANDON: Drumroll...home schooled.

CATHARINE: R UR folks religious?

BRANDON: Paranoid's more like it.

Catharine smiles at the prospect of a new friend.

CATHARINE: LOL.

BRANDON: U go to Western?

CATHARINE: Go Panthers.

BRANDON: Cool, I guess.

Debbie watches the ease with which the two communicate onscreen. Jacob slides her the keyboard. She types.

BRANDON: What do U like to do? Besides talk to cute boys on-line.

JACOB
Wait.

Jacob corrects Debbie before she can hit enter.

JACOB
Don't say that. Girls say "guys," not boys.
Language is important; say the wrong thing
and they'll know you're sketch.

Debbie BACKSPACES. She corrects, then hits ENTER.

DEBBIE
Sketch?

JACOB
Fake. Not cool.

CATHARINE: LOL. Read, bodysurf, go to the mall. Hangout mostly.

BRANDON: Sweet. One piece or two?

CATHARINE: So u can picture me in it?

BRANDON: PIR.

Catharine sits back for a moment.

DEBBIE (V.O.)
PIR?

JACOB (V.O.)
Parent in room.

BRANDON: Gotta go. ntmu.

CATHARINE: U2.

As Catharine LOGS OFF, she smiles.

Debbie looks on as Brandon logs off.

> DEBBIE
> Ntmu. Nice to meet you?

> JACOB
> You're getting the hang of it. Now you're
> connected to everyone she's ever known.
> You can basically find out everything about
> her.

> DEBBIE
> Why'd you log off? I thought things were
> going well.

> JACOB
> Cuz. Girls aren't interested in you unless
> you're ignoring them. Gotta make them
> chase you.

> DEBBIE
> That a fact?

> JACOB
> Way factual.

Debbie's look conveys a disquiet at hearing such a self aware comment
from someone more than half her age.

EXT. SCHOOL - PARKING LOT - DAY - FLASHFORWARD

Madison and Jacob are talking outside the parking lot. It's the same
shot we saw earlier, only a little closer. It feels more resonant. Even
conspiratorial.

They stand silently, but only for a moment, their hands at their side. She leans toward him to say something. It's <u>one word</u>, but we can't tell what she says. A horn HONKS. Madison bids goodbye to Jacob.

INT. SCHOOL - ADMINISTRATIVE OFFICES - DAY

Catharine sits, fidgets in her seat. Across from her—

A couple STUDENTS make inquiries of SECRETARIES. We hear an INTERCOM BUZZ. SECRETARY #1 retrieves the phone.

> SECRETARY #1
> (to Catharine)
> He'll see you now.

Catharine stands and walks over to a door. She opens it and enters. When it closes we see a PLACARD: School Psychologist.

INT. CATHARINE'S HOUSE - KITCHEN - DAY

Catharine enters as Beth cleans the kitchen.

> CATHARINE
> Mom, I need you to cut this tag off?

Beth turns to meet Catharine who turns her back to her. Beth tries to remove the clothing tag with her fingers.

> BETH
> Have to get the scissors.

Beth moves to the kitchen table where her PURSE rests. She removes her KEYS from her purse. She finds the smallest key on the ring.

She inserts the key in a CABINET DOOR. Inside we see –

SHARP OBJECTS. The block of knives, men's and women's razors, and a pair of SCISSORS, which she removes.

Beth cuts the tag off of the back of Catharine's dress.

> CATHARINE
>
> Thanks.

As Catharine leaves, Beth gives her a hug. We notice Catharine's hands remain at her side, as if physical contact makes her uncomfortable.

INT. CATHARINE'S HOUSE - LIVING ROOM - LATER

POV of Catharine lying on the sofa watching TV. We don't see what she's looking at, but the sounds of CARS and GUNSHOTS are heard.

> BOBBY (O.S.)
>
> Catharine, can you help me with my
> math?

Lulled out of her TV stupor she crosses to where her nine year old brother, BOBBY, sits doing his homework.

> BOBBY
> (reading the prompt)
> You have twelve songs on your IPOD.
> One fourth of them don't work—

> CATHARINE
> (takes over reading)
> At ninety nine cents a song, how much will it
> cost you to replace the ones that don't work?

She sets the page down, turns it over to use as a worksheet.

> CATHARINE
> How many times does four go into twelve?

BOBBY
(beat)
Four...I mean three.

CATHARINE
Okay, so multiply ninety nine cents times three.

Bobby starts writing when, the lead in his pencil BREAKS.

BOBBY
Wait. My pencil broke.

He reaches across the table and grabs a school supply pouch. Inside is a small PENCIL SHARPENER. As Bobby begins sharpening his pencil we –

CLOSE: the pencil sharpener as we watch small SHAVINGS of pencil fall on the table as a result of a TINY RAZOR inside. TILT UP TO SHOW –

Catharine taking a particular interest in the blade.

INT. MADISON'S BEDROOM - DAY

Madison sits alone in her bedroom holding her CELLPHONE. She wears a melancholy expression as if she's wrestling over something.

MADISON
(rehearsing)
Hey, Greg it's Maddie...hey Greg, it's me.
I wasn't sure if you got my messages.
Please call me back. I need to talk to you.

She dials the phone, hopeful. A couple rings later and the message box pick up.

GREG (V.O.)
This is Greg, leave a message.

Madison sinks back into her bed and cries.

> WATERS (O.S.)
> Allison here, was saying she's been feeling
> depressed lately.

INT. SCHOOL - CLASSROOM - DAY

A group of students sit around a circle as part of a PEER COUNSELLING GROUP. The advisor, MR. WATERS, sits just off to the side beside ALLISON, who looks down, not making eye contact with the others.

> WATERS
> Counselors, who here thinks they've
> felt depressed before?

> GROUP
> (various responses)
> Me...I have...yeah...been there, done that
> bought the tee-shirt.

A SLOW CIRCLE PAN around the diverse group introduces us to SEAN, ROCHELLE, TEESA, JEREMY, CLAIRE, DOUG, and MADISON.

> WATERS
> What do we mean when we say depressed?
> Teesa, what does that word mean to you?

> TEESA
> I guess feeling worthless, like I don't matter
> to anyone.

> WATERS
> Okay. Rochelle.

ROCHELLE
When I lose my appetite.

DOUG
You just described like half the girls on
campus.

ROCHELLE
Shut up!

Waters nods to Sean.

SEAN
Hi, my name is Sean and I'm depressed.

OTHERS
Hi Sean.

Laughs and giggles at the dig at AA.

SEAN
Suicide. I mean, I think about what it would
feel like, but I never actually think I'd do it.

CLAIRE
Under depression in the dictionary they
should have a picture of a teenager.

Mild laughter from the group.

WATER
Okay. Your bodies are changing against
your will, you're not sure where you belong.
        (beat)
Anyone ever have trouble sleeping?

Rochelle and Madison raise their hands.

WATERS
How often do you feel like that?

MADISON
Once in awhile. It only lasts for a few days.
But then I pick myself up.

ALLISON
You're popular though. It's probably easier.

WATERS
So popular kids can't feel bad?

ALLISON
I didn't say that—

DOUG
I know what she's saying. When you're cool
looking it's different. People want to be around
you; at least you've got a support group.

WATERS
By that logic you can tell by looking at
someone if they're depressed?

The kids kind of look to one another. Some shrug, some nod.

CLAIRE
Sometimes, yeah.

WATERS
But not always. You think some are better at
hiding it than others?

TEESA
Sure. You don't want people gossiping about
your shit.

SEAN
People meaning girls.

MADISON
Please, guys gossip just as much as girls.
(looks away, a thought occurring)

JEREMY
No, we don't gossip. We *lie*.

ROCHELLE
That's why girls can't count.

Rochelle holds her fingers about an inch apart.

ROCHELLE
(imitating a guy's penis)
"I got eight inches baby."

LAUGHTER around the circle.

BRANDON (O.S.)
Miss me?

EXT. PARK - DAY

VARIOUS SHOTS of Catharine and Brandon walking through the natural setting.

CATHARINE
(coy)
Maybe.

BRANDON
Maybe a little?

CATHARINE
Just a little.

They LAUGH.

EXT. PARK - ANOTHER SECTION - DAY

CATHARINE AND BRANDON as they walk through a park.

> BRANDON
> You're pretty easy to talk to.

> CATHARINE
> Really?

> MALE VOICE (O.S. DISTANT)
> Honey?

> BRANDON
> I was just going to check my email, see who
> IM'd. Next thing I know an hour's gone by.

She checks her watch, REACTS.

> CATHARINE
> Oh my God. My mom will kill me.

> BRANDON
> She pretty strict?

> CATHARINE
> Totally strict. She thinks the internet is too
> addictive.

> BRANDON
> I would say seductive.

Catharine looks thrilled.

> CATHARINE
> I bet the girls just can't resist you.

INT. KANARD HOUSE - HOME OFFICE - DAY - INTERCUT

Debbie sits hunched over the keyboard.

> BRANDON (V.O.)
> What other girls? There is only u.

INSERT COMPUTER SCREEN: CATHARINE: Wat about UR parents? They cool?

> TERRY (O.S.)
> Honey...?

The door opens and Terry walks in. Debbie STARTLES.

> TERRY
> There you are.

> DEBBIE
> God, you scared me. I thought you
> were Maddy.

> TERRY
> You didn't hear me calling you? I can't
> find my cellphone.

> DEBBIE
> (indicating)
> It's over there. Mine died earlier.

He walks closer to her, picks up his phone.

> TERRY
> The plumber's coming about the ceiling
> leak next week. In the meantime we're not
> supposed to use the upstairs tub.
> (beat)
> Who are you chatting with?

BRANDON: R parents ever kewl?

                    DEBBIE
          The Parley girl.

                    TERRY
          Then who's Brandon?

                    DEBBIE
          Me. I'm Brandon.

                    TERRY
          I don't understand.

                    DEBBIE
          I created him.

Off his look.

                    DEBBIE
          Brandon is trying to find out what rumors
          little Catharine is spreading about our
          daughter.

                    TERRY
          How long?

                    DEBBIE
          A couple of weeks now.

                    TERRY
          Does Madison know?

                    DEBBIE
          No, and I don't plan to tell her.

CATHARINE: They both work?

Debbie types: BRANDON: My Dad's retired—

Debbie quickly backspaces.

> DEBBIE
> No, Brandon's father can't be retired. What
> should he do for a living?

> TERRY
> You're asking me?

> DEBBIE
> Come on, it's fun.

> TERRY
> I dunno, make him an...engineer.

Debbie types: BRANDON: He's a chemical engineer.

CATHARINE: Sounds smart.

BRANDON: My rents r like cartoons. Without the funny.

> TERRY
> You're comparing me to a cartoon?

> DEBBIE
> Relax. These are Brandon's parents.

BRANDON: 2 bad he's not a chemistry teacher. He could whip us up
some really useful chemicals.

CATHARINE: UR bad.

Brandon leans in to Catharine.

BRANDON: U have no idea.

> TERRY
> I hope you know what you're doing. I'm
> going to bed.

He exits the room.

                    TERRY
          Night.

Debbie waves a hand almost dismissively. She rubs tired eyes before
continuing.

EXT. OPEN HOUSE - DAY

A SIGN outside announces an OPEN HOUSE.

INT. OPEN HOUSE - LIVING ROOM - DAY

Looking across the living room, Debbie chats with a discerning
CLIENT.

                    CLIENT
          I'd want to rip out the carpet and put
          in hardwood floors. Any idea what that
          would run?

Debbie checks her chart. The images BLUR a moment.

                    DEBBIE
          Well, factory-finished wood starts at $8
          a square foot installed, but generally runs
          $10-$14, or $1,140-$2,000 for a 12x12 space.

                    CLIENT
          Sounds pricey.

                    DEBBIE
          I've got a couple of contractors I work with
          you can talk to.

> CLIENT
> As long as they're fast and cheap.

> DEBBIE
> How soon were you looking to buy?

> CLIENT
> Oh, not for a while.

Debbie's BLACKBERRY RINGS. She's distracted by an IM:

CATHARINE: Whatcha' doing?

> CLIENT
> Is that a crack in the patio?

> DEBBIE
> (back to reality)
> Where?

The client kneels indicating a HAIRLINE CRACK in a tile.

> DEBBIE
> I hadn't noticed that before.

> CLIENT
> That kind of tile's expensive.
> (beat)
> Can we look at the upstairs?

Debbie leads her as requested.

> OPTOMETRIST (O.S.)
> Close your left eye.

INT. OPTOMETRIST'S - EXAM ROOM - DAY

Debbie sits in front of an OPTOMETRIST looking through the optical refractor.

OPTOMETRIST
Now the right.

Debbie complies.

LATER

The tests concluded, the doctor writes her a prescription.

OPTOMETRIST
Probably just eye strain. I'm going to
write you a prescription for a pair of glasses
for reading and when you're on the computer.

Debbie looks into a small VANITY MIRROR. She adjusts her new GLASSES, pinches the noseguard lightly. She shrugs, not certain she likes the image she sees.

INT. CATHARINE'S HOUSE - LIVING ROOM - DAY

Beth Parley brings laundry in to sort. Beat and –

Catharine enters through the front door. She sets her backpack down on a nearby sofa.

BETH
Hey, honey. How was school?

CATHARINE
Fine.

Catharine heads for the pantry door in the –

ADJACENT KITCHEN - INTERCUT AS NEEDED

Opens and begins perusing VARIOUS SNACK boxes.

> BETH
> How'd you do on your bio test?

> CATHARINE
> I don't know.

> BETH
> You told me he was grading them over
> the weekend.

> CATHARINE
> He didn't bring them in. Something
> about his dog ending up at the vet—

Catharine reenters with a box of snack crackers and starts to walk upstairs.

> BETH
> You're not going to your room are you?

> CATHARINE
> Uh, yeah.

> BETH
> I don't want you on urFRENZ.

> CATHARINE
> Mom—

> BETH
> You're spending all your time on that site.

> CATHARINE
> That's where my friends are.

> BETH
> Don't take that tone with me.

CATHARINE
My entire life is online—

BETH
We had an agreement. You could join but it was at my discretion as to how long you could be on it.

CATHARINE
You said I get one hour a day—

BETH
You were online for almost three hours last night—

CATHARINE
Doing homework—

BETH
—Don't lie to me. I checked your history.

CATHARINE
You're invading my privacy!

BETH
If you want to talk to that boy—

CATHARINE
His name's Brandon—

BETH
Fine. Invite Brandon over. It would be nice to finally meet him.

Catharine self consciously tugs on her RUBBER WRISTBAND.

CATHARINE
You said you wouldn't go behind my back.

                              BETH
                Don't turn this back around on me. You
                violated our agreement.

Catharine doesn't respond.

                              BETH
                Do you want me to get the contract?

Catharine YELLS as she grabs her backpack by the door.

                            CATHARINE
                I'm going to Hannah's.

                              BETH
                Dinner's at 5:30 tonight, remember. I have PTA.

Catharine exit out the door.

INT. REAL ESTATE OFFICE - DAY

Debbie preps a CONTRACT as Jacob enters, stuffing a wad of cash in
his pocket. SHARON, the agent she shares the office with, is on the
PHONE at her desk in the corner.

                              JACOB
                Hey. I got your message about a bunch of
                newsletters.

                             DEBBIE
                They're over in the corner.

Debbie returns to her desk. As she paperclips an attachment to the
contract, something on her screen gets her attention:

INSERT COMPUTER SCREEN: The urFRENZ window shows an
IM from:

CHEERIO: How do u like UR coffee?

> DEBBIE
> (puzzled)
> Do you know someone named Cheerio?

Jacob walks over. He moves up to the PROFILE section of the screen, clicks and CATHARINE'S WALL appears.

> JACOB
> It's her, she just changed her screenname.

> DEBBIE
> Why'd she do that?

> JACOB
> Because she can. Everyone does it. You
> can change your name, your avatar. Check
> this out.

He pops over to the FRIENDS section. Brings up a long screen name: SCREAMING IN SILENCE. The avatar photo is the rotting carcass of a DEAD DOG.

> JACOB
> Some kids change their name to match
> their mood or whatever.

He indicates the MOOD BOX on the screen. A HAPPY EMOTICON shows.

> DEBBIE
> How do you keep them straight?

> JACOB
> It gets confusing sometimes. That's why it's
> better to keep your setting private. Just
> in case someone's posing.

JACOB (CONT)
(beat)
Hey, am I getting paid today?

Debbie nods, types: BRANDON: With sugar, just like u.

Beat and an animated PANDA HOLDING A CUP OF COFFEE appears.

But Debbie clicks back on the image of the dead dog as we...

DISSOLVE TO:

MONTAGE

A series of shots set to MUSIC to establish the human maze that is the world of social networking. The nexus of interconnectivity that links one to many.

-Catharine's profile page.

-Catharine's list of FRIENDS. Various shots of screen names, from the normal to the abstract, intercut with faces.

-Various WORDS/HEADINGS jump out at us such as, WHAT DO YOU REALLY THINK ABOUT ME? SUBMIT ANONYMOUSLY

-PEOPLE YOU MAY KNOW.

-A link to one of Catharine's friends leads to...

-Madison's profile, her WALL. As we visit her own music and video links, we connect again to other friends, some of whom we saw on Catharine's site.

-Menu headings: HOME, MAIL, PROFILE, FRIENDS, MUSIC

-POP UP ADS and SURVEYS

-PUSH IN ON A SCREEN SHOT OF A LOCAL BAND, PSA, and...

B-ROLL FOOTAGE ALREADY SHOT: The band performs live.

BACK TO SCENE

More PHOTOS, LINKS from the networked sites.

-Submenu headings: COMPOSE, INBOX, SENT, DRAFT, SAVED

-STATUS & MOOD followed by a blizzard of EMOTICONS. From ecstatic to depressed back to euphoric, manic and angry.

As the sequence concludes, we see the above shots culminate in a frenetic blend. Until we can't tell where Catharine begins and Madison ends.

END MONTAGE:

INT. SUPERMARKET - DAY

Debbie stands in the produce sections. Removes a SHOPPING LIST from her purse. She begins selecting tomatoes. Testing them for their freshness. She tears off a PLASTIC BAG, deposits them inside.

TRACK WITH DEBBIE, as she continues shopping. She reaches—

A FEEDER AISLE

She continues turning down –

THE BEVERAGE AISLE

Debbie wheels her cart in front of a SODA DISPLAY. She seeks out a six pack of a DIET SODA. After placing it in her cart—

              BETH (O.S.)
     Debbie.

Debbie looks up to see Beth Parley.

                    DEBBIE
          Hi, Beth. How are you?

                    BETH
          Things are good. You?

                    DEBBIE
          We're fine. Jim like his new job?

                    BETH
          He likes the money. Hates the travel. There
          were some layoffs and he's having to work
          longer hours.

                    DEBBIE
          Terry's firm hasn't reached that point yet,
          knock on wood.

                    BETH
          I hear you. You finish the remodelling?

                    DEBBIE
          What a nightmare that turned out to be.

                    BETH
          Oh?

                    DEBBIE
          The upstairs bathroom. Three months
          after they installed the new copper pipes, we
          had a leak.

A couple of TEENS head down the aisle, joking.

                    DEBBIE (CONT'D)
          Had to cut through the downstairs ceiling to fix it.

BETH

That's awful.

DEBBIE

The worse part is, it's back. We'll have to
repair and repaint all over again. A mess.
            (pause)
Say, how's Catharine?

The tone of the conversation takes on a more serious tone.

BETH

Okay, I think. We found a new therapist
two months ago. He's wonderful. And
the new medication seems to be working.

DEBBIE

Good, good.
            (beat)
I was concerned when Maddy told me she
was having trouble with some girls.

BETH

Oh. When was this?

DEBBIE

Recently, actually.

BETH

            (concerned)
News to me, but then she never tells me
anything. What kind of trouble?

DEBBIE

She didn't say. Just that there was some
name calling involved. I would've called if
I thought it was anything serious.

> BETH
> No, thank you for telling me.
>> (beat)
> I should get going. I have to pick Bobby up
> from Early Birds.

> DEBBIE
> Good seeing you. Tell everyone we said hello.

> BETH
> You too.

And maybe we notice some of her pleasant demeanor has faded.

INT. DEBBIE'S CAR - STREET - NIGHT

Debbie is stuck at a stoplight in traffic. She logs onto her urFRENZ
Mobile sees an IM from:

> DEBBIE (SOTTO)
> Where R U?

Debbie starts to respond when – HONK! A horn from the car behind
her alerts Debbie to move.

INT. KANARD HOUSE - FRONT ROOM - DAY

Next morning. Debbie, in her bathrobe, reads the NEWSPAPER. She
looks up when she hears/sees –

Madison downstairs on her way to school. She looks preoccupied.

> DEBBIE
> What's wrong?

> MADISON
> Nothing.

DEBBIE
You look like something's on your mind.

MADISON
I'm fine.

DEBBIE
Is it Catharine?

Madison stops.

MADISON
What? I was over that weeks ago.

DEBBIE
Oh. Okay. Remember you have a game at three.

Madison shuts the door and exits. Debbie ponders their interaction for a beat, watches her through the front window before returning to her paper.

INT. SCHOOL - STUDY HALL - DAY

Madison works at her laptop after school. She checks out Greg's urFRENZ SITE. A SHAKESPEARE READER propped up. She gets a urFRENZ update: "This person wants to be your friend."

INSERT COMPUTER SCREEN: BRANDON: Are you OK?

Madison hits ACCEPT. Types from her own screen name:

OPHELIA1: Who is this?

BRANDON: A friend. U looked sad today. UR eyes.

OPHELIA1: Wow, somebody noticed. Better now, thanks. Greg is that U?

INT. REAL ESTATE OFFICE - INTERCUT

Debbie concludes her secret chat with Madison. She smiles, proud of herself for her anonymous attempt to cheer up her daughter.

BRANDON: Be good to yourself.

Madison REACTS with a slight but noticeable smile.

EXT. SOCCER FIELD - DAY

A game is in progress.

Madison kicks the ball through a defender's legs – then darts around her resuming her dribble.

DEBBIE

Stands on the sideline cheering her daughter on.

DEBBIE
Way to go Maddy.

Madison passes to a TEAMMATE who shoots the ball to the goal—

But the GOALIE for the other team blocks it, grabbing the ball and rolling to a stop.

MOMENTS LATER – the other teams' FORWARD dribbles the ball only to be boxed in by the defense. He tries to dribble around, but a defender KICKS the ball out of bounds. The whistle BLOWS.

The opposing team's MIDFIELDER throws the ball to a STRIKER. He takes the ball downfield and comes face to face with Madison. She sticks to him like glue.

Madison goes for a steal, but the striker fakes her out, weaves through the remaining defense, kicks and

ROCKETS the ball into the net.

The REFEREE WHISTLES TWICE indicating the end of the game.

While the other team celebrates, Madison looks disconsolate.

Debbie walks over to Madison to try to console.

> DEBBIE
> You wanna talk, honey?

> MADISON
> Leave me alone.

Madison walks off inconsolable for the moment.

HOLD ON DEBBIE looking concerned. Realizing it's time to focus attention on her own daughter.

> BRANDON (V.O)
> Are you free tomorrow?

INT. CATHARINE'S HOUSE - BEDROOM - NIGHT

Catharine lays on her stomach on the floor, homework spread around her. She looks at the laptop as she types...

CATHARINE: Why?

> BRANDON (V.O.)
> I think we should meet.

Catharine's face lights up in fear and excitement. She sits up, takes a deep breath and returns the message.

> CATHARINE (V.O.)
> Where?

INT. DEBBIE'S CAR - DAY

Debbie drives through the business area of the city.   She looks
determined, rehearsing what to say to Catharine.

> DEBBIE
> (rehearsing)
> Catharine, I'm Brandon. Don't look so shocked.
> I was upset...no, I was very upset when I
> heard you were spreading rumors
> about my daughter...don't play innocent.

INT. DEBBIE'S CAR/STREET ACROSS FROM BOOKSTORE -
DAY

Debbie is parked at the curb across the street from a bookstore. From
her vantage point, she can see clearly across the street. A light traffic
flow provides relatively unobstructed view and cover at the same time.

The dashboard clock reads 10:02A. At that, she looks back out her side
window to see –

CATHARINE

Arriving at the outdoor patio. She wears a necklace, a stylish short
sleeve top and long pants.

> DEBBIE
> You're nothing if not predictable.
> (beat; into her rear view)
> I'm Brandon. I'm...Brandon. Brandon.

Debbie looks ready to exit the car but stops. She stares out at
Catharine, watching the young girl shift nervously. And maybe Debbie
betrays a similar nervousness. Or self-righteousness. Whatever the
case, she relaxes in her seat.

DEBBIE
(cruelly)
What's the rush?

EXT. BOOKSTORE - PATIO - INTERCUT

JUMP CUTS to show Catharine passing the time. She drinks a frappucino. She leafs through a magazine trying to look occupied, dejection setting in her features as time passes.

INSERT: the DASHBOARD CLOCK reads 11:13

DEBBIE – Grows tired of watching Catharine squirm.

DEBBIE
Let's get this over with.

Debbie puts her hand on the door handle to open the door. What she doesn't see –

POV: SIDE VIEW MIRROR. A bicyclist approaching fast—

Debbie opens her door oblivious as...

The bicyclist whizzes past between her and the camera.

BICYCLIST
HEYYY!

Debbie REACTS just in time pulling back on the door, falling back narrowly avoiding a collision.

She takes a moment to catch her breath. When she does, she looks across the street to see...

Catharine is gone.

EXT. SCHOOL - DAY

The after school BELL SOUNDS. Students begin exiting.

EXT. COFFEE SHOP - DAY

Establish a local java hut.

INT. COFFEE SHOP - DAY

A popular caffeinated hang out for adults and teens.

At the counter, Catharine takes her COFFEE from the Barrista.

CATHARINE
                 Thanks.

She walks across to her seat where her school books rest alongside her
LAPTOP.

Catharine OPENS her HISTORY text and begins typing up notes for
an exam. Beat –

Her INSTANT MESSAGE alert flashes. It shows BRANDON'S
name.

INSERT COMPUTER SCREEN: BRANDON: You're not a very
good friend.

Catharine REACTS looking confused. She hurriedly begins typing her
response <u>under her new screen name</u>.

OVRJOYD: Are U joking.

BRANDON: U talk a lot of shit.

CATHARINE (V.O.)
What are you talking about? Where were you
yesterday? I waited over an hour?

BRANDON (V.O.)
I heard you spread rumors about Madison's
sex life.

CATHARINE (V.O.)
Madison Kanard? U know her?

The shop door opens and a CLASSMATE enters. Recognizes her.

CLASSMATE
Hey, Catharine.

Catharine looks up, almost alarmed.

CATHARINE
Oh, hi.

CLASSMATE
You get your English Paper back?

CATHARINE
Yeah, I got a B plus.

CLASSMATE
Levin gave me a B. I can't complain; I wrote
it in like an hour the night before.

Catharine checks her screen again, nervous. Sees a new response from
Brandon.

INSERT COMPUTER SCREEN: BRANDON: She goes to my
church.

The flashing CURSOR on the IM begging for her response, matches
the beating of her heart.

The classmate notices her open book.

>   CLASSMATE
>   History. I hate that class.

>   CATHARINE
>   (perturbed)
>   Tell me about it. We have a test tomorrow.

>   CLASSMATE
>   Well, good luck.

She turns away from her. Catharine dives back into IMing.

OVRJOYD: She told you that?

She looks up and BRANDON is seated across from her.

>   BRANDON
>   People in the youth group.

>   CATHARINE
>   It was a joke. I told like one person.

>   BRANDON
>   Doesn't sound very LOL to me.

>   CATHARINE
>   I heard a guy say it.

>   BRANDON
>   Which guy?

>   CATHARINE
>   I don't know.

>   BRANDON
>   Because it's not true.

CATHARINE
You've got it wrong. I'm not like that.

BRANDON
Then why'd you do it?

Catharine looks distressed now, the conversation affecting her.

CATHARINE
Last year she told me she didn't want to
be friends anymore. She was popular, I'm
not, end of story.

Brandon's image has disappeared.

INSERT COMPUTER SCREEN: BRANDON: Whatever.

INT. REAL ESTATE OFFICE - DAY

Jacob finishes typing away at the keyboard, Debbie hovering over him.

CATHARINE: Brandon don't be like that.

Debbie reaches over, CLICKS OFF leaving Catharine in limbo.

JACOB
Why'd you log off?

DEBBIE
Because she's lying.

Sharon enters from the front door.

SHARON
Debbie, I need you to do me a huge
favor. My mother's back in the hospital

                              DEBBIE
                    Sharon, I'm so sorry—

                              SHARON
                    It's okay. I've got everything under control
                    except for the Kennedys. They're signing
                    their loan docs this afternoon, and they're
                    gonna drop them through the night slot. It's
                    important that you get them to the lender
                    by 5:00 tomorrow, otherwise I'm gonna lose
                    my rate lock, okay?

                              DEBBIE
                    Sure thing.

HOLD ON Jacob, looking pensive as he stares at the screen.

EXT. KANARD HOUSE - NIGHT

We juxtapose shots of the two homes...

EXT. PARLEY HOUSE - NIGHT

A collision imminent.

INT. SCHOOL - CLASSROOM - DAY

Madison slumps in her seat while a history teacher, MR. DOUGLAS,
drones.

                         MR. DOUGLAS
                    When is it wrong to publicize the truth about
                    someone? (beat) In the mid to late nineteenth
                    century, many people began to believe they
                    had by necessity two selves, one public and one
                    private. They had to address the problem of

MR. DOUGLAS (CONT)
justifying or explaining why something private
should become public knowledge.

Madison's not paying attention, too busy inking Greg's name on the
inside of her left forearm.

MR. DOUGLAS
We see this in literature where certain types of
writing position the reader as a voyeur,
someone transgressing the writer's private life.
In epistolary fiction, letters or journals are used
to publicize the private through the agency of
print. In such works, a letter could be both direct
and sincere, or deceptive and performative. The
fin de siècle blackmail fiction of Conan-Doyle
and Raymond Chandler was born out of the notion
of the split self. Warren and Brandeis, writing for
the Harvard Law Review in 1890, declared
that "instantaneous photographs and newspaper enterprises have invaded the sacred precincts
of private and domestic life

The irony of the lecture is lost on the classroom as students trade texts
and tweets from their hardware devices.

MR. DOUGLAS
...and numerous mechanical devices threaten to
make good the prediction that "what is whispered
in the closet shall be proclaimed from the house-
tops." The issue has never been more applicable
than today in the age of the World Wide Web.
With so much information, both public and
private, accessible at the click of a mouse, the
question remains: is privacy a right or privilege?"

Madison crosses off Greg's name as if coming to a conclusion.

EXT. SCHOOL - QUAD - DAY

End of the school day. Madison walks through the quad when her RINGTONE SOUNDS. She answers her phone: an IM awaits.

INSERT CELLPHONE SCREEN: BRANDON: Sorry u lost.

Intrigued, Madison returns the text, CLICKING her message.

OPHELIA1: I didn't know you cared.

BRANDON: More than you know.

Madison looks up to see Jacob approaching, his cellphone out.

INT. EXT. DEBBIE'S CAR/SCHOOL - PARKING LOT - DAY

Later, Debbie pulls into the parking lot to see –

Madison and Jacob talking, their cell phones held across from one another blutoothing. The same shot we saw earlier but in real time.

Madison leans toward him to say something. We can't hear what she says. A horn HONKS. She bids Jacob goodbye.

Jacob walks over to Debbie at the car.

> DEBBIE
> What were you two talking about?

> JACOB
> Nothing.

> DEBBIE
> I told you I don't want you discussing
> Catharine—

JACOB
We just exchanged email addresses.

Debbie relaxes, hands him a batch of OPEN HOUSE fliers.

DEBBIE
Here are the fliers. I need them distributed
after school today.

EXT. MALL - DAY

A local outdoor mall.

Brianna pulls over in her car. Madison rides beside her, Courtney in the
back seat.

BRIANNA
I ate too much at lunch.

COURTNEY
Tell me about it. I could barely buckle up.

MADISON
You guys, we only had half a salad.

BRIANNA
Must be my period.

Madison gets out of the car, the girls following.

BRIANNA
Anyone have change.

MADISON
(checking her purse)
I think I have some dimes.

COURTNEY
Plastic only, sorry.

BRIANNA
I hate paying for parking.

Madison hands over her change. Brianna starts to plug them into the meter, notices it's broken.

BRIANNA
Broken. Crap, what do I do now? Can we still park here.

MADISON
We should look for another space.

BRIANNA
Where? Back in the scary parking lot where some guys will try to rape us.

MADISON
You wish.

Brianna snickers.

COURTNEY
They towed my brother's car. Then they charged him like twenty dollars to impound it.

BRIANNA
Sucks. What do I do?

MADISON
Just leave a note on the windshield. Maybe you'll be okay.

COURTNEY
I have a pen.

Courtney fishes a pen from her purse, hands it over. While Brianna
fishes her own purse for paper.

> BRIANNA
> Court, did Matt call you about the concert?

> COURTNEY
> It's not going to happen.

> MADISON
> Please. He's told like half the campus he
> likes you.

Brianna starts writing a note.

> COURTNEY
> I can never tell.

> BRIANNA
> What, if a guy's into you?

> COURTNEY
> My guy-dar sucks. The signals are so confusing.
> Like the whole touching thing. I mean, so many
> times I'll see a girl lying on the quad with her
> head in some guy's lap, or she's kissing him
> on the cheek and it turns out they're just friends.

> MADISON
> Or friends with benefits.

> BRIANNA
> Don't they teach you this in Wisconsin?

> COURTNEY
> I think they're more concerned with animal
> husbandry.
>   (laughing)

Brianna sticks the note on the windshield.

TRACK

the girls as they enter the main shop area.

> COURTNEY
> I saw this cute necklace at the mall the other
> day.

> BRIANNA
> That reminds me, I've got to find a pair of
> pearl earrings.

> MADISON
> You need *another* pair?

> BRIANNA
> My stupid sister dropped one in the toilet the
> other day.

> MADISON
> Casey's always in my stuff.

> COURTNEY
> Doesn't your Mom do anything about it?

> MADISON
> Yeah, right. She's in there more than Casey.
> Looking for stuff.

> BRIANNA
> Remember when she found that condom in
> your backpack?

> MADISON
> Total meltdown. I told her the school hands
> them out like candy.

COURTNEY
You should've told her Brianna gave it to you.

BRIANNA
Shut up, bitch.

A cell phone RINGS. All 3 girls check their phones. Madison opens her looking a little too hopeful.

MADISON
Hang up.

BRIANNA
Would you stop?

MADISON
What are you talking about?

BRIANNA
I saw that look. Could you possibly be any more desperate?

Madison comes clean.

MADISON
So what if it was him?

BRIANNA
It's been two months already. Move on.

COURTNEY
You really think it's Greg?

MADISON
That's the vibe I'm getting. He's not using his real name, but...

Madison comes to a halt before a shop window, the others following suit.

> BRIANNA
> Of course it's Greg. Who else could it be. That's
> what he does, play games. He dumped you once,
> he'll dump you again—

> COURTNEY
> She's PMSing, don't listen to her. I think you
> guys will totally get back together.

> BRIANNA
> (to Courtney)
> Stop coddling her. That's the last thing she
> needs.
> (to Madison)
> He doesn't deserve you.

> MADISON
> Maybe he's changed.

> BRIANNA
> Look, you're my friend, so don't take this
> the wrong way, but we're here for you. Greg—

> COURTNEY
> Brianna—

> MADISON
> I can't believe you said that.

> BRIANNA
> (to Courtney)
> And don't pretend you don't feel the same
> way.

> MADISON
> Wait. You guys talk behind my back?

Courtney looks guilty.

BRIANNA
I'm sorry. I'm not the type to stand by and
watch this happen again. I can't do it.

MADISON
So, this is what...an intervention.

BRIANNA
We're trying to help you.

MADISON
You're supposed to support me.

COURTNEY
We don't want to see you get hurt again.

BRIANNA
Look, we've been best friends for forever,
okay. But you need to respect that. Stop
being so selfish. Think about what we've
had to go through these last few weeks.
Watching you beat yourself up. We're tired
of it.

Madison looks like she's fighting to keep it together.

COURTNEY
We miss the old Maddy.

MADISON
(tearing up)
What's the matter with me? I never did
anything to him. He dumped me for no
reason.

BRIANNA
He's a guy. Guys are dicks. They're all dicks
if they get the chance. It's like a math equation.

                              COURTNEY
                   I think you mean a syllogism.

                               BRIANNA
                 Whatever. Wait—did you just say jism?

She laughs a beat. Realizes Madison's not laughing.

                               BRIANNA
                 We're your friends, okay. We just want you
                 to be happy. Okay?

Madison shrugs, puts on a brave face.

                               BRIANNA
                 Hugs.

Beat, and the three girls come together in a hug.

                              COURTNEY
                 Can we please go shopping now?

Madison nods. The girls continue to walk off.

EXT. CONVENIENCE STORE - DAY

Jacob removes an OPEN HOUSE sign from the lot adjacent to the
property.

He tosses it into the back of his car.

INT. CONVENIENCE STORE - DAY

Jacob enters and walks to the Slurpee-type machine. He doesn't see
Catherine enter the store and walk out of frame.

He walks over to the counter placing his drink down.

CASHIER
Dollar seventy nine.

Jacob reaches into his pocket for his wallet but comes up empty. He begins fishing CHANGE out of his pocket. It CLATTERS onto the counter. Jacob counts it up.

JACOB
Forgot my wallet. Only have a buck and
a quarter.

The Cashier gives him a look –

CATHARINE (O.S.)
Wait. I think I have it.

Jacob turns to see Catharine standing behind him holding a candy bar.

JACOB
You don't have to—

CATHARINE
No big. It's just money.

She finds fifty cents in change and finishes paying.

EXT. CONVENIENCE STORE - DAY

Catharine exits the store. Jacob is waiting for her. And maybe we detect a hint of guilt in his expression.

JACOB
Thanks.

CATHARINE
You go to Western, don't you?

> JACOB
I'm a senior.

> CATHARINE
I think I've seen you before. I'm Catharine.

> JACOB
Br...Jacob. Jacob Ross. You live around here?

> CATHARINE
A few blocks south.

> JACOB
Cool.

An awkward pause follows.

> CATHARINE
I-I gotta get home.

> JACOB
I'll pay you back next time I see you.

Catharine gets on her bike.

> CATHARINE
No worries. Bye.

Catharine rides off. As she disappears around the corner...

Jacob has a thought, suddenly pursues her.

> JACOB
Wait up.

Catharine looks over her shoulder, surprised. She comes to a stop. Jacob catches up to her. He continues to walk with her as she lazily bikes alongside.

INT. CATHARINE'S HOUSE - BEDROOM - NIGHT

Catharine looks anxious as she sits curled up on the floor, her eyes open, listening to music on her IPOD. The door opens and her mom enters.

> BETH
> Catharine?

She opens her eyes. Removes her headphones.

> CATHARINE
> What?

> BETH
> Can I talk to you for a minute?

Catharine sits up. She seems unusually sensitive.

> CATHARINE
> My homework's almost finished—

> BETH
> I want to talk about Brandon.

> CATHARINE
> Mom—

> BETH
> I think it's affecting your school and your attitude at home.

> CATHARINE
> My attitude—

> BETH
> You come home from school and go straight to your room—

                        CATHARINE
            We already went over this—

                          BETH
            You spend all your time on urFRENZ.

Catharine just shrugs. A long silent beat.

                          BETH
            How well do you know this boy? He doesn't
            go to your school.

                        CATHARINE
            He's homeschooled. I think his parents
            are super religious. Can we stop talking about
            this?

                          BETH
            You get really quiet when I ask you about him.
            Do you know why that is?

Catharine clams up.

                          BETH
            I don't want you getting careless online:
            TMI, remember? Too much information.
            I want all your setting back to private by
            tomorrow morning. Clean it up or I'm
            cancelling your account.

Catharine MUMBLES under her breath.

                          BETH
            I didn't catch that.

                        CATHARINE
                        (annoyed)
            I said, okay. Jeez.

Beth leaves closing the door behind her. Catharine rolls her eyes, returns to her headphones and her music.

INT. CATHARINE'S HOUSE - STUDY - NIGHT

Beth sits behind closed doors finishing her QUICKEN books. She suddenly stops what she's doing and brings up urFRENZ on the internet window.

She LOGS onto Catharine's site and copies Brandon's address. She then logs onto her own page. She IM'S Brandon.

BETH: I'd like a word with you.

She hits ENTER. Beat and she returns to her bookkeeping.

LATER

Beth is busy number crunching when she gets an IM.

BRANDON: Who is this?

Beth responds typing: BETH: Beth Parley, Catharine's mother.

INT. KANARD HOUSE - HOME OFFICE - INTERCUT AS NEEDED

Debbie REACTS as she sees Beth's name on the screen.

BRANDON: Heyy.

BETH: How old are you, Brandon?

BRANDON: 17. Why?

BETH: I'm curious about all Catharine's friends.

BETH: Where do you live?

Beth waits in lengthy silence.

BRANDON: How well do u know UR daughter?

> BETH (ALOUD)
> What kind of question is that?

BRANDON: Maybe she's not who u think she is.

> BETH (ALOUD)
> The nerve of this kid.

Beth is taken aback. She tries to remain calm.

BETH: Who do you think she is?

BRANDON: Im not the one spying on her.

> BETH (ALOUD)
> Oh, I do not like you, Brandon.

BETH: Maybe you should let me be the parent.

BRANDON: Whatever.

Beth looks fit to be tied. Beat and she types...

DEBBIE

sits at her desk as Beth's final message appears.

BETH: I don't want you communicating with my daughter anymore.

Debbie pauses for a second, considering what to say. Then just LOGS OFF.

>   BETH (O.S.)
>   Can't the police do anything?

INT. CATHARINE'S HOUSE - LIVING ROOM

DETECTIVE DOUG JAMES, his BADGE hanging from his coat pocket, sits across from Beth and her husband, JIM. It's informal, like a friend of the family.

>   DET. JAMES
>   ...I hear you Beth. My Jennifer's the same
>   age as Catharine. But this kid, Brandon,
>   from what you've told me no actual crime
>   has been committed.

>   BETH
>   What if he's not a kid? He sounds older.

>   DET. JAMES
>   Predators may spend months trying to groom
>   a victim. They can be hard to spot, but there
>   are some warning signs. Does he focus too
>   much attention on your child's emotions?
>   Are they unusually sympathetic—

The cop's pager goes off. Beth looks to Jim.

>   DET. JAMES
>   I've got to take this.

>   JIM
>   I appreciate you dropping by Doug. We just
>   feel so helpless.

>   DET. JAMES
>   No problem.
>   (beat)

                    DET. JAMES (CONT)
Why not just cancel her account? That's what
I'd do.

                         BETH
Believe me, I've come close several times. But
she gives me so little anyway. It's the only way
I can find out anything about her.   That and she
hasn't cut since she's been on it.

                    DET. JAMES
I don't envy you.

EXT. CITY - DAY

Various shots of Catharine riding through city.

EXT. LIBRABY - DAY

TRACK Catharine riding up to the library, locking her bike.

INT. LIBRARY - COMPUTER WING - DAY

Catharine sits in front of a computer.   Her trig book is beside her but
it's obvious by the look on her face that she's having trouble
concentrating.

She logs on to urFRENZ. She's changed her name (Melancollie) and
Avatar again. Sees there are NO NEW MESSAGES.

She COMPOSES a new text to Brandon:

MELANCOLLIE: U there?

A long, agonizing beat. She stares at the screen like a watched pot hoping to will a message on the screen. Precious moments later and one appears.

BRANDON: I cant talk to u any more.

MELANCOLLIE: What do u mean?

EXT. HART PARK - RIVERBED - DAY

Catharine stands at a distance from Brandon.

                          BRANDON
              I mean it's over.

                          CATHARINE
              Are you serious?
                    (beat)
              Tell me what's wrong.

                          BRANDON
              Besides the fact you're a liar and you spread hate.

Catharine types furiously.

                          MELANCOLLIE (V.O.)
              I'm not a liar!

                          BRANDON (V.O.)
              Ask your Mom.

EXT. CATHARINE'S HOUSE - BACKYARD - DAY

Beth and Jim, relax in a HOT TUB. They chat over glasses of wine when Catharine storms outside.

CATHARINE
Mom, what did you do?

BETH
What are you talking about—

CATHARINE
Brandon doesn't want to talk to me any more.
He said to ask you.

Beth sighs. Looks to her husband.

CATHARINE
I knew it!

BETH
I chatted with him last night online.

CATHARINE
(hurt; angry)
You're not supposed to be on urFRENZ.

BETH
We had an agreement that if I felt there was
something suspicious—

CATHARINE
There's nothing suspicious!

BETH
—I would have the right to do so.

CATHARINE
He's not a child molester. Jesus, Mom! Take
a Xanax why don't you.

JIM
Don't talk to her like that!

                         BETH
            You don't even know him—

                       CATHARINE
                       (teary eyed)
            I know I like him! Why won't you let me be
            happy?

                          JIM
            We've every right to be concerned.

                         BETH
            He doesn't sound like a typical teenage boy—

                       CATHARINE
            He's not. That's why he likes me!

She stomps off upstairs in tears.

Beth is left to hang her head.

INT. CATHARINE'S HOUSE - BEDROOM - DAY

A SERIES OF JUMP CUTS: Catharine paces back and forth in her
room clearly agitated. Biting her nails. Pressing her hands tightly
against her ears, her eyes closed.

INT. CATHARINE'S HOUSE - BATHROOM - DAY

Catharine races towards the toilet, drops to her knees and VOMITS
into the bowl.

CATHARINE – sits with her back to the wall, crying.

MEDICINE CABINET – she reaches for her antidepressants and takes
2 pills.

CATHARINE – her knees tucked up against her chest, rocks back and forth in an effort to calm herself. We hear a KNOCK on the door followed by Beth's Voice: "Catharine, open up."

INT. JACOB'S HOUSE - GARAGE - DAY

Jacob sits off to the side close to the main garage door. He's watching a COMEDY SITE on Youtube, counting his money. Beat and –

He clicks on another image behind it. The sounds of a COUPLE FUCKING. We don't see the porn, but the accompanying GRUNTS and GROANS leave nothing to the imagination.

Jacob watches. He looks almost bored. As if he's seen so many images he's become desensitized to it. We hear the sound of a CAR pull up in the driveway. Beat—

We hear the car door CLOSE. The sound of HIGH HEELS nearing.

                    JACOB'S MOM (O.S.)
          Jacob.

                         JACOB
              In here.

His mom, RUTH, late 30's, pokes her head in.

                         RUTH
               What are you doing?

                         JACOB
              Looking at porn.

Jacob nonchalantly clicks off the image leaving the comedy website the only thing visible onscreen.

                         RUTH
               Ha ha. Where's your brother?

                            JACOB
              I don't know, in his room probably.

                             RUTH
              Would you go check on him while I get
              dinner ready?

INT. JACOB'S HOUSE - LIVING ROOM - DAY

A short while later. Jacob lies on the floor next to his brother BEN, 7.
They play an older racing video game.

                             BEN
              I wish we had better games.

The two MANIPULATE their controllers guiding their respective
racers on the screen.

                            JACOB
              You're going too fast on that turn.

                             BEN
              Dakota has a GameTron. We played golf
              on it last week.

                            JACOB
              Dakota's dad didn't get laid off.

                             BEN
              You think Dad's ever going to get another
              job?

Ben's racer skids off the track.

                             BEN
              I hate when it does that.

                              JACOB
            That's cuz' you didn't listen to me. You always
            cut your speed when you're coming to that turn.
            You have to look at what's ahead of you.

Ben buckles down as his racer is returned to the track.

                         JACOB'S DAD (O.S.)
                              (calling)
                         Jacob, phone call.

Jacobs gets up. Ben continues playing.

                              JACOB
            Push pause you little cheater.

Ben pushes pause. Jacob tousles Ben's hair on the way out. As soon as
he does, Ben pushes play and continues the game.

FRONT ROOM

Jacob enters the adjacent room to find his dad, MIKE, sitting at a
LAPTOP reading about home based businesses. He hands Jacob the
CORDLESS PHONE.

EXT. SUBURBAN STREET CUL-DE-SAC - DAY

TRACK WITH JACOB as he skateboards through the asphalt streets
of a city block, a cul-de-sac. Wears a BACKPACK.

He CURB HOPS onto the sidewalk and up –

A DRIVEWAY to a house. He stops when he comes to the front
walkway. Removes a REALTOR NOTEPAD from his backpack and
drops it on the front porch.

He turns, hops back on his board and skates towards the next house.
CONTINUE TRACKING –

As Jacob skates over to the next house. He stops his board in front of the lawn. He walks across the grass and places the notebook in the MAILBOX.

Jacob HOPS the curb again, then dismounts as his board stops at the edge of the lawn. He walks up to the house, deposits a notepad when he overhears—

>   MADISON (O.S.)
>   How come you never call me?

>   GREG (O.S.)
>   There's nothing to say. Look, I've got
>   practice.

Through the GLASS of the front door, <u>Jacob sees Madison talking heatedly to Greg Barnes.</u> Jacob freezes trying not to call attention to himself.

>   MADISON
>   Why'd you go out with me in the first place?

>   GREG
>   I don't know, I thought you were different.

>   MADISON
>   What do you mean *different?*

>   GREG
>   Let it go Maddie.

>   MADISON (O.S.)
>   What'd you say happened at the party?

>   GREG
>   What do you think I said?

                    MADISON
          You haven't called me back. You just hide
          behind a text screen.

                    GREG
          I'm not the one hiding— We broke up. We're
          done.

Jacob lingers for a beat, then retreats back to his board.

EXT. CONVENIENCE STORE/STREET - DAY

CLOSE an OPEN HOUSE SIGN is posted in a grassy area outside a
convenience store.

A frustrated Jacob pulls the sign out of the ground. He walks...

Over to his CAR, a HATCHBACK. He pops the lock on the rear,
lifting the back to reveal a stack of other signs. He tosses the sign in –

SLAMS the hatchback preparing to leave.

INT. RESTAURANT - DUSK

A popular Mexican eatery. Debbie, her husband, Madison and Casey,
await their food as a BUSBOY drops off a bowl of chips.

                    CASEY
          I want the red chips.

Casey starts to reach across –

                    DEBBIE
          Wait your turn.

Debbie passes the chips towards her husband, who puts them between
Madison and Casey. Madison grabs a RED CHIP.

CASEY
That's not fair, I get the red chips. Mom!

MADISON
Casey—

Debbie hands Casey her CELLPHONE with a Tetris game on it.

DEBBIE
Here, play the bricks.

TERRY
I think I'm going to have the carnitas.

A WAITER arrives with their drink order. As he does, Debbie hears her PHONE VIBRATE in her purse. She retrieves.

WAITER
Margarita on the rocks no salt.

He puts Debbie's drink down in front of her, then her husband's drink in front of him.

WAITER
One cherry coke, and one root beer.

DEBBIE checks her blackberry. Someone's sent a text with a PHOTO attached. She clicks to open and reaches for her DRINK.

WAITER
Are you ready to order, senor?

Casey sees something of interest on the CELLPHONE.

CASEY
Mommy, you've got pictures!
(beat)
Who's this?

Debbie REACTS to whatever she's been sent. So does Madison who reaches for the phone –

                    DEBBIE
          No!

Quickly, Debbie snatches the phone from Casey's hands.

                    MADISON
          What's your problem?

Debbie is speechless as she tries to regain composure.

                    TERRY
          You okay?

                    DEBBIE
          It's...just spam.

INT. KANARD HOUSE - DINING ROOM - NIGHT

Debbie sits alone at the table. Drowning her thoughts in a bottle of wine. Madison enters. Looks like she's finally ready to open up to her Mom about what she's been feeling.

                    MADISON
          Mom, can I talk to you?

                    DEBBIE
          Can it wait 'til morning?

Madison opens her mouth to say something, thinks better.

                    MADISON
          Never mind.

She walks back out of the room. Debbie checks her CELL PHONE again in disbelief. Looking alarmed. Maybe even scared.

INT. REAL ESTATE OFFICE - DAY

Jacob clicks over to see –

It's an IM from Catharine. He double CLICKS. Beat and –

A NUDE PICTURE COLLAGE of Catharine appears. Jacob is taken aback at first.

The SEXTING PHOTOS include a shot of Catharine sitting up, her naked back to the camera, a sheet covering the rest of her.

>   DEBBIE (O.S.)
>   She sent this to me last night when I was
>   at dinner. With my family.

The second shot is of her lying on her belly, her bare back, maybe the crack of her ass exposed.

The third shot is of her on her back in bed, upside down in the frame. And maybe this is the most disturbing as she awkwardly tries to look sexy.

We see IMAGES in quick bursts: her breasts, her navel, her pubic region.

Debbie looms behind him.

>   DEBBIE
>   What's wrong with that girl?

Angry, Debbie quickly LOGS OFF.

>   DEBBIE
>   Did you tell her to send that?

>   JACOB
>   No!

                              DEBBIE
          She just decided to send nude photos of herself
          to you.

                              JACOB
                Obviously.

                              DEBBIE
          There's nothing obvious about it, except that
          girl has something wrong with her.

Debbie looks visibly shaken by this.

                              DEBBIE
          What's the matter with you? Don't you have
          any respect for yourselves?

Debbie considers this new development.

                              DEBBIE
                      (accusatory)
          You sure you didn't ask her to send this? I can
          check the history to find out.

                              JACOB
                      (angry)
          This wasn't exactly in my job description.

Debbie walks away in disgust. Jacob looks clearly perturbed.

SHARON

Debbie's office partner, enters. She looks on edge.

                              SHARON
          Did you get those loan docs over to the bank
          yesterday?

                        DEBBIE
                      (realizing)
               Sharon, I am so sorry.

                        SHARON
               They might lose the house now—

                        DEBBIE
               I can't believe I forgot. I was going to swing
               by on the way home—

Jacob opens a new pack of NOTEPADS to deliver trying to disappear.

                        DEBBIE
               What can I do? Let me call the mortgage
               broker—

                        SHARON
               There's another offer on the table. If the owner
               takes it, I'm fucked.

                        DEBBIE
               I'll make it up to you I swear.

                        SHARON
               Is something the matter at home? Because lately,
               even when you're here, you're not here.

Sharon tires and exits. Debbie can only hang her head.

INT. SCHOOL - UPSTAIRS HALLWAY - DAY

TRACK with Catharine as she walks alone down a long hallway.

INT. SCHOOL - CLASSROOM - DAY

While a TEACHER lectures –

Catharine sits at her desk. She bites what's left of her fingernails. She looks anxious as she checks her phone for text messages.

CELL PHONE SCREEN: No new messages.

EXT. SCHOOL - ATHLETIC FIELD - DAY

Catharine jogs listlessly around the track.

INT. CATHARINE'S HOUSE - KITCHEN - DAY

The Parleys are having a quiet dinner.

> CATHARINE
> May I be excused?

> BETH
> You've hardly eaten.

> CATHARINE
> I'm not hungry.

Beth looks to Jim. He shrugs, indicating his reluctant approval.

> JIM
> Is this still about that Brandon?

> BETH
> It's not about Brandon. It's about her.

INT. CATHARINE'S HOUSE - BEDROOM - DAY

Catharine enters hurriedly closing the door behind her. She LOGS ONTO urFRENZ looking...hopeful.

But the look on her face changes as the CHAT FEATURE on her urFRENZ MAILBOX page appears revealing a string of comments:

INSERT COMPUTER SCREEN: BRANDON: What were u thinking sending those to me?

BRANDON: Where's UR self respect?

> BRANDON (V.O.)
> Don't send any more pictures.

Catharine suddenly looks lonely. Scared.

> BRANDON (V.O.)
> Don't ever contact me again.

INT. KANARD HOUSE – MADISON'S BEDROOM - NIGHT

Madison sits at her desk typing on her computer, homework spread out. She's wearing her IPOD. Beat and the door opens revealing her Dad.

> TERRY
> You seen your Mother?

No response.

> TERRY
> (louder)
> MADDY!

She heard that. She turns, lifting her headset.

> TERRY
> You seen your mother? The bank's calling
> about a bounced check.

> MADISON
> I think she's at the office.

                                   TERRY
                          At this hour? Christ!

He closes the door. Maddy returns to her typing.

INT. REAL ESTATE OFFICE - NIGHT

A stressed out looking Debbie works on a real estate deal.

                                  DEBBIE
                    Hey, Jodie. We must've gotten our signals
                    crossed about the open house. Does Sunday
                    work?... Can we come around 11:30?... Great.
                    I'll see you at 11:30, then.... No, I'll be there.
                    Alright, thanks.
                              (hangs up, relieved)

Her Gmail link notifies her of an incoming message. She clicks on it:

MADGIRL16: Why RU avoiding me?

                                  DEBBIE
                              (beyond irritated)
                    Goddammit. Catharine. Overjoyed,
                    cheerio, mellancollie, madgirl. This girl is a
                    mess.

Debbie counters with a terse, angry response.

INSERT COMPUTER SCREEN: BRANDON: Your words mean
nothing to me.

BRANDON: Everything you say is a lie.

Debbie sits at her desk obsessing.

MADGIRL16: I've never done anything to u.

BRANDON: Another lie.

MADGIRL16: ASSHOLE.

MADGIRL16: I thought u liked me.

BRANDON: What's to like? UR an empty vessel.

INT. SCHOOL - CAFETERIA - DAY

Jacob enters. He passes other STUDENTS surfing for food and friends.

CONTINUE TRACKING as he beelines for a display near the register. He selects a packet of POP TARTS and a bottle of KERNS NECTAR. PAN ACROSS to –

THE REGISTER

Jacob steps up behind a student who finishes paying the CASHIER. He slides his purchases across.

TRACK with Jacob as he passes MADISON and a group at their table that include Brianna and Courtney. In front of them...

VFX: their urFRENZ NAMES appear on screen: BRIANNA24, COURT32, EGGMAN, ANGRYBUNNY, DBOY310. We recognize some from their avatars on both Madison and Catharine's urFRENZ pages.

CAMERA LINGERS as we hear snippets of their conversation.

                    MADISON
          Do we have a game this weekend?

                    COURTNEY
          Yes, totally sucks. You going to Kirby's
          party?

                    MADISON
          Of course I'm going.

                    BRIANNA
          I'm planning on getting so wasted.

                    COURTNEY
          I thought you were still under house arrest.

                    BRIANNA
          Whatever, I'll just sneak out.

                    EGGMAN
          Once I got so hammered after I snuck out, I
          couldn't find my own house.

                    ANGRYBUNNY
                    (laughs)
          I remember that.

                    MADISON
          You like, woke up on some guy's front
          porch.

A GROUP OF JOCKS walks by Madison's table. Including STEVE-O
and WOODMAN.

                    EGGMAN
          Steve-O, don't forget the thing at Kirby's.

                    STEVE-O
          I'll be there.
                    (acknowledging)
          Ladies.

CAMERA CONTINUES TRACKING with the Jocks.

                        STEVE-O
            What time does practice end?

                        WOODMAN
            When coach decides we've had enough. Pro'lly
            around five.

                        STEVE-O
                        (beat)
            Have to get the truck washed this weekend.

They walk out of the auditorium.

EXT. SCHOOL - QUAD - DAY

TRACK with Steve-O and Woodman as they pass a row of classrooms.

                        WOODMAN
            My Dad's talking about going out to the desert week
            after next.

                        STEVE-O
            Taking the bikes.

                        WOODMAN
            Of course.

                        STEVE-O
            Alright, later.

Steve-O splits from Woodman and enters –

INT. SCHOOL - LIBRARY - DAY

A quiet room where students meet with student and adult TUTORS.
Steve-O takes a seat across from a student, KIM.

                    KIM
          Didn't think you were gonna show today.

                    STEVE-O
          Sorry I'm late. Lost my cell phone two days
          ago and I've just been winging it.

                    KIM
          It's cool. How are you doing in Robertson's
          class?

                    STEVE-O
          Better, I think. But I'm still a little lost on
          the whole imaginary numbers concept.

Kim points to a problem in a TEXT BOOK.

                    KIM
          Let's try this.
                    (indicating)
          Simplify the square root of negative five.

Steve looks at the problem. Starts jotting down solutions.

Beat and a TATTED UP PUNK sets down his book from across the
room, and walks toward us. TRACK WITH HIM as he exits into—

EXT. SCHOOL - QUAD - DAY

Continue TRACKING as he slides his HEADPHONES over his ears.
SPEED METAL practically threatens to burst his eardrums. He pulls
out a CELLPHONE and checks his messages as he walks.

Tat Punk's boots STOMP their presence through the halls. He turns right down a corridor and enters into –

INT. SCHOOL - CAFETERIA - DAY

CONTINUE TRACKING as he passes a table full of GAMERS. He nods to one of them, RYAN; they fist bump as he passes. Stay with the gamers as they discuss a card game strategy.

He displays a CARD. Other PLAYERS chime in.

> BIGGEEK 1
> What about Faeries?

> DORKOIL
> They're useless against Cloudthreshers.

> RYAN
> You can't beat his 7/7 instant speed
> monstrosity.

TILT UP to show Catharine and Hannah passing them, holding trays of food.

CAMERA TRACKS with them as they weave their ways through tables and stop at a table along the far wall. They sit and begin to eat their lunch. Catharine doesn't recognize –

JACOB as we RACK FOCUS. He sits across the room from her observing her briefly, before he goes back out of focus.

> HANNAH
> You watch the show last night?

> CATHARINE
> Just the first part. Then I had to do homework.

> HANNAH
> Hayley has an amazing voice.

> CATHARINE
> Tell me about it. I think she could win.

> HANNAH
> Maybe. Damon's cuter.

> CATHARINE
> Too bad he's gay.

> HANNAH
> He still could win.

Suddenly there is the sound of cell phones RINGING or BUZZING throughout. It starts in the far corner and works its way toward us along with an accompanying commotion. A STUDENT BUZZ follows: "oh my god," "she's hot," and LAUGHING.

Student heads turn instinctively to look at the source. Their interest builds from table to table like a wave until it stops at –

> CATHARINE
> Something's happening.

Catharine's table. Hannah's phone VIBRATES. She picks it up. Flips open the phone.

> HANNAH
> It's a text message.

Catharine is now aware of the interest being directed at her table. She looks around her as if to confirm the buck stops with her. Beat and...

> HANNAH
> Oh my god.

Catharine grabs the phone from her. She sees –

CLOSE: Her nude PHOTOS on display. Realizes they've been texted around the student body.

She drops the phone. Quickly gets to her feet amidst the catcalls, laughter and pity sighs. She walks away, calmly though hurriedly at first, before breaking into a dead run.

She bursts out of the cafeteria into daylight.

EXT. SANTA ANA RIVERBED - DAY

Humiliated, Catharine runs through the wash.

She finally slows to a halt. Gathers herself and SCREAMS into the day. A long beat as she pours out her angst.

Her cell phone RINGS. She retrieves it. Whatever the message, the look on her face says it's not good.

INT. REAL ESTATE OFFICE - DAY - LATER

Debbie typing as Brandon on urFRENZ.

INSERT COMPUTER SCREEN: BRANDON: UR such a liar. Everyone says so.

MADGIRL16: WHO!

Debbie looks over at a PHOTO COLLAGE of an older soccer photo. Of Madison and Catharine from two years ago. And their teammates. We recognize Brianna, maybe another girl.

BRANDON: Danielle, Brianna, Hannah, Wendy, Holly, Riley.

MADGIRL16: I dont believe u.

BRANDON: You know its true.

MADGIRL16: Stop sayin that.

> BRANDON (V.O.)
> You are a bad friend.

MADGIRL16: Dont. I would die for my friends.

> BRANDON (V.O.)
> PROVE IT!

Beat. A long one as she hits DELETE SELECTED FRIENDS on the urFRENZ page. She SLAMS her hand down on the desk with an air of disgust, finality.

Jacob enters.

> DEBBIE
> Jacob, good you're here. I want you to delete
> Brandon. I can't do this anymore.

INT. CATHARINE'S HOUSE - HALLWAY - DUSK

Catharine exits her bedroom. She looks down, forlorn, as she heads into the bathroom. Closes the door behind her.

INT. CATHARINE'S HOUSE - BATHROOM - DUSK

Catharine looks into the mirror. Doesn't look like she's too happy with the image staring back at her.

> BETH (O.S.)
> Catharine! Phone call.

She opens the door.

> CATHARINE
> Who is it?

> BETH (O.S.)

Hannah.

> CATHARINE

I'll-I'll call her back.

She shuts the door. Reaches into her pocket and removes —

THE PENCIL SHARPENER we saw earlier. A long beat.

Catharine starts SNAPPING the rubber band around her wrist. It finally breaks. She presses the blade to the flesh of her forearm, begins to cut. Deep.

INT. KANARD HOUSE - KITCHEN - DUSK

Debbie serves the food on Madison's plate. Casey calls to her from somewhere in the house.

> CASEY (O.S.)

Can we eat now?

> DEBBIE

In a minute. Is your sister down yet?

> CASEY (O.S.)

No. She's still upstairs. Your phone's vibrating.

Debbie washes her hands at the sink.

INT. KANARD HOUSE - HOME OFFICE - DUSK

Debbie enters to find a TEXT from Jacob on her phone.

INSERT BLACKBERRY: I won't be coming into work anymore. Keep last weeks pay. I told Catharine.

Before she can react, a DROP OF WATER, hits her hand. She looks up to see it's coming from the spreading ceiling stain.

INT. KANARD HOUSE - UPSTAIRS HALLWAY - DUSK

Debbie, shaken, walks down the hallway to see the bathroom door shut, light coming from beneath it. EMO MUSIC playing low from behind the door.

> DEBBIE
> Madison, don't turn the water on in the tub.
> The leak is back. Anyway, dinner's on.

She's about to head back downstairs when she notices Madison's bedroom door open, her laptop cracked open on her desk.

INT. KANARD HOUSE – MADISON'S BEDROOM - DUSK

Debbie enters. She lifts the laptop cover. She's not prepared for what she sees.

INSERT COMPUTER SCREEN: MADISON'S WALL REVEALS...

BRANDON: UR a bad friend. MADGIRL16: Dont. I would die for my friends. BRANDON: PROVE IT.

The conversation has been posted on her BULLETIN to all. Other FRIENDS have chimed in with like RANDOM INSULTS.

Debbie's memories come rushing back to her...

INT. SCHOOL - PARKING LOT - DAY - FLASHBACK - INTERCUT

Madison and Jacob are talking as before. She leans toward him to say something. It's <u>one word</u> --

>   DEBBIE (O.S.)
>   What were you two talking about?

BACK TO SCENE

Debbie replays another conversation in her head.

AUDIO MEMORY HIT: JACOB at the office.

>   JACOB (O.S.)
>   Lemme guess, your daughter has an account
>   and you want to spy on her?

BACK TO SCENE

Debbie looks perturbed. Something's really bothering her.

AUDIO MEMORY HITS:

>   JACOB (O.S.)
>   You can change your name, your avatar.

Debbie, a mental dawning approaching...

>   JACOB (O.S.)
>   Some kids change their names to match their mood.

>   MADISON (O.S.)
>   Mom, can I talk to you?

>   DEBBIE (O.S.)
>   Overjoyed, cheerio, mellancollie, madgirl.

PARKING LOT

Madison and Jacob. She says something to him, one word. And this time we hear it. <u>Her urFRENZ name.</u>

MADISON
MADGIRL16.

BACK TO SCENE

A heartskipping beat and Debbie goes rigid at the horrible realization that <u>her last few days of hurtful communiques have been with her own daughter</u>.

She looks outside the open door to the closed bathroom door.

INT. KANARD HOUSE - HALLWAY - DUSK

Debbie rushes to the bathroom door, KNOCKING ON IT.

> DEBBIE (O.S.)
> Madison, are you in there?

Debbie tries the doorknob.

> DEBBIE
> (with greater urgency)
> Open the door!

Debbie shoves then SHOULDERS the door open. Her SCREAM quickly follows as we see—

> DEBBIE
> OH JESUS!

INT. KANARD HOUSE - BATHROOM - DUSK

DEBBIE'S POV: Madison lying in the bathtub filled with blood.

Debbie rips the shower curtain aside. Water SLOSHES as she struggles to wrestle Madison's body from the tub between brief bouts of screaming.

She turns over Madison's wrists: two VERTICAL SLASH MARKS.
On the ledge of the tub is a RAZOR BLADE.

                    DEBBIE
          No no no...
              (yelling)
          CALL 911.

                    CASEY (O.S.)
          What's wrong?

                    DEBBIE
          Your sister hurt herself. DO IT!

She rocks Madison in her arms, barely conscious of the tears running
down her face.

                    DEBBIE
          Baby hang on. Hang on.

INT. CATHARINE'S HOUSE - LIVING ROOM - DUSK

Beth has set the table. The whole family is gathered except for
Catharine. They hold hands preparing to say grace.

                    JIM
          What's keeping her?

                    BETH
              (calling)
          Catharine! We're waiting on you.

                    JIM
              (a long beat)
          Maybe I should see...

An interminable beat. Finally, we hear a door OPEN. FOOTSTEPS follows and Catharine enters.

                    CATHARINE
          Sorry.

She sits, they hold hands.

                      FAMILY
          Bless us oh Lord for these thy gifts we're
          about to receive. Amen.

They begin eating dinner.

                       JIM
          This tri-tip is delicious.

The phone RINGS in the background. Beth pushes her chair back and disappears into the kitchen to answer.

                              FADE TO BLACK.

FILMMAKER Q&A

The following is a sampling of topics that have been discussed while I was exhibiting "@urFRENZ" in film festivals across the country:

Q: Your film deals with the rift between parents and teens over cyberspace. What do you think is the cause of it?

A: We're now dealing with a generation of children that have never known a world without an internet. As parents, I think that at least subconsciously, we're all a little frustrated because we remember a simpler time when our jobs might have been a little easier. We not only have to parent over our kids in terrestrial space, but cyberspace as well.

Kids have traditionally had a limited worldview, one shaped and governed by adults at home or in school. But the internet changed that. They can now enter a world with near equal access as grownups. They have time on their hands, which allows them to master that world quickly, often more quickly than adults. Additionally, it's a world more in line with their constantly changing attention spans and one in which they develop a sense of entitlement.

Q. Did you set out to make a "message film?"

I wanted to make a film that served as a talking point to help bridge the latest generational divide between parents and kids. To me, a message film is akin to someone standing on a soapbox and lecturing people. In writing the script, I tried to remember what it was like to be a teenager. I knew that I wouldn't want to be preached to so I wasn't going to proselytize or speak down to my audience.

Q. What advice would you give to parents about monitoring their children's cyberspace?

A. The Internet is an adult responsibility. Treat it as one. Explain to your kids that in order for you, as parents, to utilize the web, you must sign contracts and agree to the terms of use with the hardware, software and wireless companies providing your service. If they want access to the internet, the same rules need to apply to them. Prepare a contract for them explaining the uses of their access for both the computer and cell phone. With stiff consequences, like loss of internet or computer privileges, if they don't.

Q. Do you think parents should spy on their kids' private internet conversations?

It's important that you establish and maintain a level of trust with your child. They need to know they can come to you if there is a problem. Go online with your kids. Establish a safe environment. But don't forget, you're a parent first. Respect their privacy, but if you believe your child to be at risk of predators or bullies, access their history, check their sites. A blog or social networking site is not a diary. It's an invitation to discourse. And you, as a parent, have the final say.

I recommend keeping the computer in an open room, with younger children especially. You can monitor their activities either by yourself or with commercially available programs or services that prevent them from entering unauthorized sites.

MAIN CREDITS

Brookwell McNamara Entertainment
Presents

A Virtually Exposed Production

@urFRENZ

Lily Holleman
Gayla Goehl
Najarra Townsend
CaroleAnne Johnson
Michael Robert Kelly
And James Maslow

Bree Essrig
Ryann Kidd

Jana Winternitz
Nikki Limo

Bernard X. Kopsho
Paul Carafotes
Billy St. John
Charlotte White

Music by Lisbeth Scott

Music Supervisor Diane Burk

Casting by WinPhil

Director of Photography J. Soren Viuf

Production Designer Kristy Winter McCaw

Editor Zachary Anderson

Executive Producers The Phillips Brothers
Michael & Elaine Gallagher

Executive Producers David Brookwell
Sean McNamara

Co-Producer Michael J. Gallagher

Produced by Jana Winternitz

Written and Directed by Jeff Phillips

END CREDITS

CREW

Music Performed, Recorded, and Mixed by	Lisbeth Scott
Visual Effects Producer	Billy Peake
@urFRENZ Website Designer	Jessica Lares
Associate Producer	Matthew Sullivan
Special Visual Effects	Nick Guth
1st Assistant Director	Shannon Marie Welch

CAST

Catharine Parley	Lily Holleman
Debbie Kanard	Gayla Goehl
Madison Kanard	Najarra Townsend
Beth Parley	CaroleAnne Johnson
Jacob Ross	Michael Robert Kelly
Brandon	James Maslow
Hannah	Bree Essrig
Greg	Ryan Kidd
Brianna	Jana Winternitz
Courtney	Nikki Limo
Teri Kanard	Paul Carafotes
Teacher	Billy St. John
Casey	Charlotte White
Jim Parley	Bernard X. Kopsho
Ruth Ross	Annette Phillips
Bobby Parley	Sean Fitzgerald
Steve-O	Robb Steinhauser
Zoe	Emmeline Kim
History Student	Vanessa Wolf
Partyers	James Pabst
	Shad Harris
Kid in classroom	Michael Sheppard
Secretary	Christina Sawyer
Sharon	Danielle C. Carlson
Real estate client	Mary L. Juhasz
Student seen several times in the film	Matthew Sheppard
Ben Ross	Donovan Phillips
Peer Counselors	Devyn Howard
	Mona Molayem
	Sophie Nikfarjam
	Jocelyn R.C.
	Chris Donnelley
	Mackenzie Stith
	Shayna Stuart
	Kyle Cooper

	Amir Malaklou
Mr. Waters	Patrick Sullivan
Police Officer	Patrick Vincent Upstill
Soccer referee	Chris Juhasz
Soccer players	Brooke Springer
	Kelsey Rustigan
	Brooke Elby
	Melissa Laxamana
	Shauna Salcido
	Lexa Glantz
	Lauren Young
	Taylor Ramirez
	Kelly Mitsumori
	Shelby Osborne
	Monique Cherry
Soccer fans	Arnette McCrimmon
	Aida Castro
	Genevieve Phillips
	Celeste Phillips
MIA Girl's Gym Teacher	Christina Welsh
Optometrist	Dr. Janice Jackman
Kendama	Itself
Social Networking Language Consultants	Kelley Logan
	Shaena Brun
	Jamie Ford
Dracula & Rights to Privacy consultant	Dr. Logan Esdale
Storyboards Artist	Billy Peake
PSA Band	Jeremy Gonzales
	Mathew Sheppard
	Geoff Sullivan
	Aaron Geiser
	Gabriel Castro
Camera Operator	J. Soren Viuf
Additional Camera Operators	Michael Nie

	Brandon Alperin
	Eric Ulbrich
1st Assistant Camera	Emanuele Parrini
Additional First Assistant Camera	June Zandona
	Ian Barbella
	Bret Watkins
	Boa Simon
2nd Assistant Camera	Jocelyn R.C.
Additional 2nd Assistant Camera	Dillon Morris
	Alicia Pharris
	Niels Lindelien
Steadicam Operator	Justin Browne
Still Photographer	Shannon Marie Welch
Digital Imaging Technician	Eric Ulbrich
Digital Imaging Technician	Dillon Morris
Digital Imaging Technician Assistant	Clinton Noel Williams
Sound Mixer	Chad Tomlinson
Gaffer	Cory Reeder
Best Boy Electric	Yuki Noguchi
Key Grips	Ramin Shakibaei
	Kyle J. Good
Best Boy Grip	Chris Donnelley
Dolly Grip	Nick Erickson
Grips	Alicia Pharris
	Kiko Suura
	Ronald Drynan III
	Adrian Fernandez
	Rafael Cobos Delgado
Assistant Costume Design	Emmeline Kim
Assistant Production Design	Matt Crawford
	Scott Borg
Soccer Wardrobe	Vicki Gray

John Gray

Makeup Artists	Rachel Galey
	Ceciley Jenkins
	Melissa Anchondo
	Ganita Berry
Script Supervisors	Sabrina Parke
	Candice E. Smith
Location Manager	Matthew Sullivan
Assistant Location Manager	Billy Peake
Production Coordinator	Amber Dubeshter
Production Accountant	David Noone
Assistant to Miss Winternitz	Sloane Hayes
Assistants to Mr. Phillips	Rachel Skidmore
	Amanda Young
Production Assistants	Rafael Cobos Delgado
	Emmeline Kim
Extras Wrangler	Edie Sheppard
Soccer Wrangler	Jane Mitsumori
Video game design	Ben Peake
@urFRENZ Logo Design	Ibrahim Dilek
Post Production Supervisor	Zachary D. Anderson
Post Production Sound	Mike Robertson
Foley Artist	Tricia Robertson
Assistant Sound Editor	Ian Beckman
Cello Soloist	Tina Guo
Digital Intermediate Colorist	Tashi Trieu
Craft Service	Amber Dubeshter

Legal Services	Donald V. Smiley
Electric Equipment	Evolution Image Group
	Evidence Productions
Camera Rentals	Hollywood Camera
	Acey Decy
Grip Equipment	Gear Monkey
	Wooden Nickel

'Youth" by White Apple Tree
From Velvet Mustache CD
Courtesy of 37 Records

"Government Child"
Performed by Capra
Courtesy of Capra Inc.

"Rat Thompson"
Performed by PM Nightly
Courtesy of Fervor Records, a division of Wild Whirled Music

"Rat Thompson"
Written by Patrick Michael McGarey

"Butch"
Written by Saint Motel
Performed by Saint Motel
Courtesy of On The Records

"Crucial"
Written and Performed by Lisbeth Scott
Published by Tofu Cat Music
Courtesy of Zone Records/Whistling Bird Music

"Nothing"
Written by Ashlee Morton
Performed by Ashlee Morton

"U Never Know"
Written and Performed by Lisbeth Scott
Published by Tofu Cat Music
Courtesy of Zone Records/Whistling Bird Music

"Whatever"
Performed by Najarra Townsend
Courtesy of Najarra Townsend

"Tangled"
Written and Performed by Lisbeth Scott
Published by Tofu Cat Music

"Another Day"
Written and Performed by Lisbeth Scott
Published by Tofu Cat Music
Courtesy of Zone Records/Whistling Bird Music

"Modern Life"
Written and Performed by August House

SPECIAL THANKS
Chapman University & Dodge College
Dean Bob Bassett
David Kost
Michele Kennedy
Dan Leonard

FILMED AT
City of Orange
Orange High School
SK Johnson
City of Fullerton Public Library
Timothy Mountain
WorldStar Global Real Estate Services
Mike and Loretta Kenney
Sandra and Bob Polk
Maria Foscari

Dr. Janice Jackman
Hart Park
7/11
Chapman Coffee Shop
City of Santa Ana
City of Huntington Beach

The Producers Wish To Thank
To Annette, my wonderful wife, for always supporting my artistic
endeavors. I love you
My children, Gabriel, Aida, Donovan, Genevieve, and Celest
Jim Strader and Quattro Media
Sparkler Entertainment
Charles Segars
Christina Welsh
Brian Haberlin
Anthony Cistaro
Sean McNamara
Dan Markle
Bruce Johnson
Steve Duncan
Dana Long
Lois Walker
David Brookwell
Cheryl McDowell
Yoram Ben-Ami
Terilyn HIllis
Scott Allen
Marilyn Peake
William Peake
Melissa Purner
Michael & Elaine Gallagher
Sarah Mohen
David Stein
Renny Valencia
Caroline Godin
Max & Diana Enscoe
Tami and Bill Winternitz

Stacey Kattman
Billy Hufsey
Dan Parsons
Dona and Nelson Phillips
Greg and Glenn Phillips
Tina and Jon
Bob Jones & Carla O'Neill
Orange Soccer Club Premier White GU17
Jim Blaylock
Burr and Nancy Anderson
Lauren McKeithan
Totally Sketch.com
Mahalo.com
Roberts family
Robertson family
Simeon Greenstein
Jon Robertson
Patrick O'Sullivan
Richard Ryan
Conrad Quilty Harper
Dave Eaton
Ryan J. Budke
Sloane Hayes

A Film By: Everyone Who Worked On It!

No animals were harmed during the making of this film

FOR AIDA

ABOUT THE WRITER - JEFF PHILLIPS

Jeff Phillips began writing for features and television in 1995. He is a ten time produced screenwriter and a member of the Writer's Guild of America. His debut script, King's Ransom, was a political action thriller for Disney. Since then, he has split his time between writing big budget action and science fiction flix and more intimate family fare for both film and television. He is also a published novelist and has written two graphic novels. Jeff is a graduate of Loyola Marymount University and Chapman University. He lives in Huntington Beach, California, with his wife Annette and their five children.